M257 Unit 10
UNDERGRADUATE COMPUTING

Putting Java to work

'lets do Java

Unit **10**

This publication forms part of an Open University course M257 *Putting Java to work*. Details of this and other Open University courses can be obtained from the Student Registration and Enquiry Service, The Open University, PO Box 197, Milton Keynes MK7 6BJ, United Kingdom: tel. +44 (0)870 333 4340, email general-enquiries@open.ac.uk

Alternatively, you may visit the Open University website at http://www.open.ac.uk where you can learn more about the wide range of courses and packs offered at all levels by The Open University.

To purchase a selection of Open University course materials visit http://www.ouw.co.uk, or contact Open University Worldwide, Michael Young Building, Walton Hall, Milton Keynes MK7 6AA, United Kingdom for a brochure. tel. +44 (0)1908 858785; fax +44 (0)1908 858787; email ouwenq@open.ac.uk

The Open University
Walton Hall, Milton Keynes
MK7 6AA

First published 2007. Second edition 2008.

Edited, designed and typeset by The Open University.

Printed and bound in the United Kingdom by Hobbs the Printers Ltd.

ISBN 978 0 7492 1995 6

2.1

The paper used in this publication contains pulp sourced from forests independently certified to the Forest Stewardship Council® (FSC®) principles and criteria. Chain of custody certification allows the pulp from these forests to be tracked to the end use (see www.fsc-uk.org).

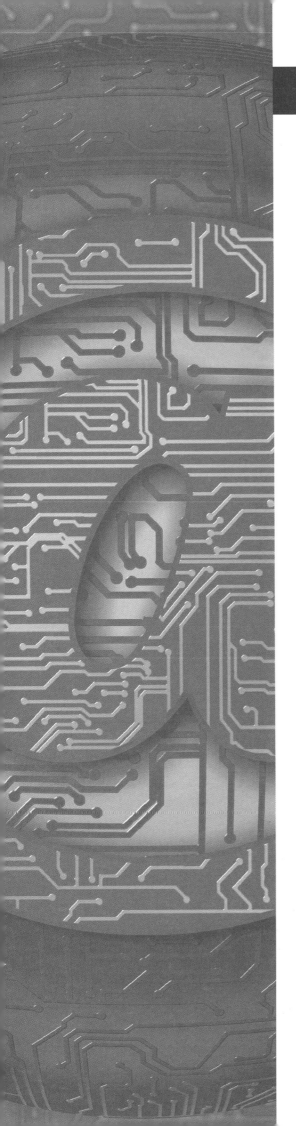

CONTENTS

1 Introduction 5

2 Applets 6

   2.1 How an applet works 6

   2.2 How to write an applet 7

   2.3 The applet life cycle 10

   2.4 An applet example 12

   2.5 The security restrictions on applets 16

   2.6 When to use applets 17

   2.7 Problems with browsers 18

3 MIDlets 20

   3.1 Configurations and profiles 21

   3.2 MIDlets 22

   3.3 The **Displayable** class 25

   3.4 High level interfaces 26

   3.5 Low level interfaces 36

   3.6 Persistent storage 40

   3.7 Networking MIDlets 40

   3.8 MIDlet packaging 41

4 Servlets 43

   4.1 What is a servlet? 43

   4.2 How do servlets work? 44

   4.3 A simple example of servlet coding 46

   4.4 Using a servlet to respond to user input 49

   4.5 Servlets and JSP 52

   4.6 Servlets and databases 54

5 Aglets 56

   5.1 What is an aglet? 56

   5.2 Mobility 56

   5.3 Host servers and the server context 57

   5.4 Aglet life events 58

   5.5 Aglet applications 58

6 Hardware Java 60

   6.1 Embedded systems 60

   6.2 Embedded systems example 63

   6.3 Java Card 65

7 Review 67

8 Summary 70

   Index 72

M257 COURSE TEAM

M257 *Putting Java to work* was adapted from M254 *Java everywhere.*

M254 was produced by the following team.

Martin Smith, Course Team Chair and Author

Anton Dil, Author

Brendan Quinn, Author

Janet Van der Linden, Academic Editor

Barbara Poniatowska, Course Manager

Ralph Greenwell, Course Manager

Alkis Stavrinides, External Assessor, Coventry University

Critical readers

Pauline Curtis, Associate Lecturer

David Knowles, Associate Lecturer

Robin Walker, Associate Lecturer

Richard Walker, Associate Lecturer

The M257 adaptation was produced by:

Darrel Ince, Course Team Chair and Author

Richard Walker, Consultant Author and Critical Reader

Matthew Nelson, Critical Reader

Barbara Poniatowska, Course Manager

Ralph Greenwell, Course Manager

Alkis Stavrinides, External Assessor, Coventry University

Media development staff

Andrew Seddon, Media Project Manager

Garry Hammond, Editor

Ian Blackham, Editor

Anna Edgley-Smith, Editor

Jenny Brown, Freelance Editor

Andrew Whitehead, Designer and Graphic Artist

Glen Derby, Designer

Phillip Howe, Compositor

Lisa Hale, Compositor

Thanks are due to the Desktop Publishing Unit of the Faculty of Mathematics and Computing.

1 Introduction

The underlying theme of this course is that Java is a highly portable programming language and is able to run on a very wide range of platforms.

This means that Java software may be required to run on very small scale systems with few resources, such as very limited storage or very small displays, as well as on large networks of powerful servers with very extensive hardware resources. To cater for these very different environments, we have the concept of **Java editions**. So far, we have mostly been concerned with the Java 2 Standard Edition (J2SE). In this unit, we will look at Java 2 Micro Edition (J2ME), designed for use on smaller systems with limited resources, especially the concept of **MIDlets**, applications which run on so-called Mobile Information Devices. Large scale systems are catered for by the Java 2 Enterprise Edition (J2EE), which we will consider only briefly in this unit. Fortunately, many of the concepts we have met in the previous units apply to all Java editions.

On networked systems, including clients and servers, there is the additional question of where the Java software is located and where it is executed. In this unit, we will see that there are many possible answers to this – in a complex system, Java software may run on the client, on the server (possibly as a **servlet**), as an **applet** invoked from a web page, or even as a software agent (an **aglet**) roaming around the network. Typically, a system will use an appropriate combination of such Java software components.

In this unit, we aim to:

▶ show how to write applets and when to use them;

▶ demonstrate and apply the J2ME concept of MIDlets, to produce software for small scale devices;

▶ discuss the idea of servlets, running on a web server;

▶ briefly explain software agents, or aglets;

▶ show how Java is used in a variety of embedded devices, such as smart cards or printers.

First, we look at applets, which are Java programs invoked from a web page.

2 Applets

In the very early days of the Java language – all the way back in 1995 – the most exciting thing was that Java could be used to add animation, processing and interactivity to web pages. Until then, most web pages had been more or less static, with just the possibility of a bit of form-filling as the most dynamic activity on offer.

Very early demonstrations at conferences and across the web involved many animations of steaming coffee cups as well as more ambitious graphical displays. This was all achieved by means of **applets**, which are Java programs that are downloaded as bytecode along with a web page and run by the browser when the web page is viewed. Since those early days, things have moved on – there are other ways of making web pages more interactive (such as the JavaScript language); processing for web-based applications can be done more efficiently in many cases (using servlets and Java Server Pages); there are also strong competitors for graphics and animation (such as animated GIF files or various proprietary graphics and animation products).

The designers of Java also deliberately restricted what applets are normally allowed to do – for example, they usually cannot access files on the client computer where they are executed. This is because you generally should not trust programs that you download from the web, perhaps unknowingly, by simply clicking on a web link.

Nevertheless, applets can be very useful and their security features can be an advantage in some cases. In this section, we will explain when to use applets and how to write them.

2.1 How an applet works

In many ways, a Java applet is similar to a Java application. In both cases, you write Java source code, compile it to bytecode and store it in a file with a name ending in `.class`. The difference comes in how this bytecode file is then invoked and executed. An application is typically installed directly on a particular computer and run there although, as we shall see later, it may be invoked from a remote computer. When an application is run, the bytecode is interpreted and executed by the Java Virtual Machine (JVM) on the computer where the application resides.

By contrast, the bytecode for an applet is normally run when an associated web page is loaded into a browser. If the web page is loaded from a web server on a remote computer, then any applet bytecode linked to that web page is also downloaded and run.

The applet bytecode is actually interpreted and executed by a suitable web browser – a so-called Java-enabled browser. The sequence of events in the process of downloading and executing an applet is illustrated in Figure 1.

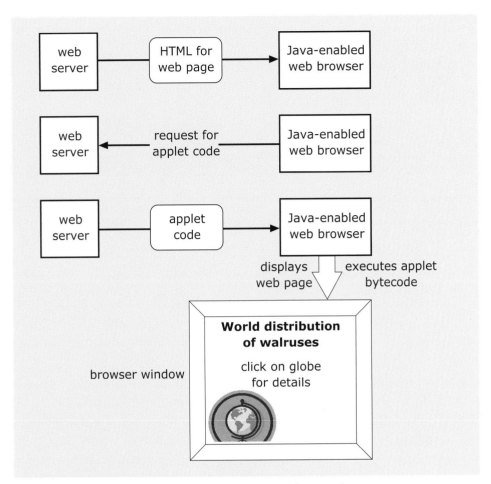

Figure 1   Sequence of events showing how applets work

As the name 'applet' suggests, an applet is typically a small piece of code, but it need not be, as long as users are prepared to wait for a larger applet to download along with its associated web page. In most cases, users will not want to wait, so limiting applets to manageable size is a good aim.

Applets can also be viewed using a standard application called the `appletviewer` – this comes as part of the JDK, the freely available Java Development Kit. This is often useful for testing during development of an applet.

2.2   How to write an applet

In order to write an applet, you must first define a class that extends the `Applet` class from the `java.applet` package or its subclass `JApplet` from the `javax.swing` package.

You will be pleased to know that much of what we have covered already about writing applications also applies to writing applets. Applets can use almost all the Java language features and most of the API components we have previously seen. There are a few key differences, however, between applications and applets because applets must run in conjunction with a web page. These are as follows.

▶ An applet does not have a `main` method. It has an `init` method, which is invoked by the browser when the web page is loaded.

▶ Applets have a graphical user interface only, and use normal Swing or AWT features for this. When running in a browser, they cannot read or write using the standard streams such as `System.out`.

▶ For the applet GUI, you do not need to construct a `Frame` or `JFrame` object, as the browser window is used instead.

▶ An application with a GUI may use the `setSize`, `setTitle` or `setVisible` methods of the `Frame` class. For applets, sizing is done in the HTML file; they cannot have title bars and they are made visible automatically.

This means that it is quite straightforward to convert a simple graphical application into an applet. Here is a simple applet that displays a label containing a familiar message:

```
import java.awt.*;
import javax.swing.*;

public class HelloWalrusApplet extends JApplet
{
    public void init()
    {
        Container pane = getContentPane();
        JLabel label = new JLabel("Hello Walrus");
        pane.add(label);
    }
}
```

The applet is a subclass of `JApplet`, which is a standard class from the Swing library. It defines one method, `init`, which is automatically run when the applet is first loaded, such as when you first view the associated web page.

Before we can run this simple applet, we need an HTML page. This can contain any normal HTML tags and other content, but must also contain a special tag that links the web page to our applet. Traditionally this is the role of the `<APPLET>` tag, logically enough, you might think. Here is some suitable HTML:

Note that except for the `<HR>` tag, each HTML tag has its corresponding closing tag starting with a slash '/'.

```
<HTML>
    <HEAD>
        <TITLE>Testing the Applet HelloWalrusApplet</TITLE>
    </HEAD>
    <BODY>
        <H1>A message for walruses everywhere</H1>
        <HR>
        <APPLET CODE="HelloWalrusApplet.class" WIDTH=400 HEIGHT=300>
        </APPLET>
        <HR>
    </BODY>
</HTML>
```

This contains a few items of standard content – a title for the web page, a piece of text that is displayed in large font (because of the `<H1>` tag), and two `<HR>` tags that cause the applet to be enclosed by two horizontal lines (horizontal 'rules'). The `<APPLET>` tag has three parameters, specifying the location of the compiled code for the applet together with the width and height in pixels of the applet window on the screen.

Finally, to run the applet, we can use a Java-enabled browser (which we shall discuss further later) or perhaps, at this stage, the `appletviewer` program. We supply the name of the HTML file (not the applet file) to the `appletviewer` program and it displays just the applet window, ignoring the rest of the HTML. The result should be similar to that in Figure 2.

Figure 2   Running a simple applet using the `appletviewer` program

Using a browser to view the applet gives quite a different result, as shown in Figure 3.

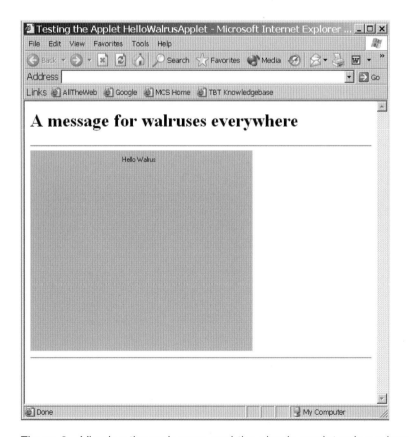

Figure 3   Viewing the web page and the simple applet using a browser

Now we see the effect of the HTML tags and other contents of the web page. The applet is shown in a window of size 400 by 300 pixels, as specified in the `<APPLET>` tag.

This reinforces the point made earlier – the `appletviewer` is very useful for checking the applet by itself during development. For final testing of how the applet will look when its web page is displayed, you must use a browser. For an applet to be made widely available, you will need to test it using different browsers and browser versions, as there are quite a few differences in how browsers support various features of applets. We shall discuss this in a later subsection.

HTML tag options for applets

In more recent versions of HTML (since HTML 4.0), the `<APPLET>` tag has been deprecated and we are expected to use the `<OBJECT>` tag. Unfortunately, older versions of browsers are not aware of the change, so we have to decide whether to comply with HTML 4.0 (and perhaps have to accept that our applets do not work on some browsers) or to continue to use `<APPLET>` tags, which are recognized on all browsers apart from very ancient ones. The choice depends on how widespread you expect the use of the applet to be. If it is only to be available within a limited environment, such as an Intranet, then you may be able to ensure that all the browsers can cope with `<OBJECT>` tags. In this unit, we will continue to use the `<APPLET>` tag.

2.3 The applet life cycle

We have seen how to write a very simple applet, with only an `init` method. This method is invoked to initialize the applet when it is first loaded, normally when you first view the web page that links to the applet. In this sense, the `init` method acts like a constructor, and should be used for activities that need to be performed once in the lifetime of the applet. We would not normally put all the code for an applet into the `init` method.

For more complex applets, it is useful to have more control over whether the applet continues to run when the user is no longer viewing the related web page. The applet life cycle methods, shown in Table 1, are useful in this case. It is important to note that these methods will be invoked by the browser or `appletviewer` – they should not be invoked explicitly by the code for your applet. For example, when a web page with a linked applet is first viewed using a browser, the `init` method of the applet will be invoked, followed by the `start` method.

Table 1   Applet life cycle methods

Method	Description
init	invoked when the applet is loaded, e.g. when the applet web page is first viewed
start	invoked when the applet is made active, e.g. when the user applet web page is viewed (possibly again)
stop	invoked when the applet is made inactive, e.g. when the user moves away to view a different web page
destroy	invoked just before the applet is unloaded, e.g. when the user closes down the browser or `appletviewer`

The applet inherits the life cycle methods, which are shown in Table 1, from its superclass `Applet` and these methods should be overridden, if required. The superclass methods typically do nothing. Let us consider when you might need to override one or more of these methods.

The `init` method and the `destroy` method are each invoked once during the lifetime of the applet, but the `start` and `stop` methods may be invoked several times if the web page is revisited. If an applet uses significant processor resource when running, such as might occur with a complex animation, it is good practice to implement `start` and `stop` methods. This ensures that the processor is only being used when the web page is viewed. The `init` method should be used for one-off initialization, such as allocation of resources, like defining arrays and initializing instance variables. The `destroy` method is less commonly required, especially since Java garbage collection deals with releasing memory resources. However, it should be used for any final clean-up operations or releasing of resources before the applet terminates. Figure 4 illustrates the sequence of events.

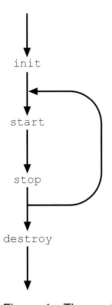

init

start

stop

destroy

Figure 4   The applet life cycle

For example, an applet that uses threads would typically use the `init` method to create the threads and the `destroy` method to finally remove them. The `start` and `stop` methods might start and suspend execution of the threads respectively.

There are a few other important methods for applets, and these are listed in Table 2.

Table 2   Other important applet methods

Method	Description
`paint`	invoked to draw the applet window graphical contents (executed when the applet window appears or is changed)
`isActive`	returns true if the applet is active, an applet is marked *active* just before its `start` method is called and is marked *inactive* just before its `stop` method is called
`resize`	requests a new size (in pixels) for the applet window – use with caution for applets to be viewed using a browser, as the size specified by the `<APPLET>` tag defines a maximum size
`getImage`	retrieves an `Image` object from a specified URL; this image can then be displayed on screen
`getAudioClip`	retrieves an `AudioClip` object from a specified URL; this audio clip can then be played
`play`	plays the `AudioClip` object to be found at a specified URL

The abstract class `Image` is the superclass of all classes that represent graphical images. The `AudioClip` interface is a simple abstraction for playing a sound clip. See the API for details.

Among these methods, the most frequently used is the `paint` method, which is invoked by the system to draw the applet window and any graphical content it may have. You may need to override the `paint` method that is inherited from the `Applet` class, to define the graphical content of your applet window. This is particularly useful if the graphical content is to be dynamic. The next subsection shows an example of this.

The other methods in the table are useful for checking whether the applet is still active, for changing the size of the applet window from the size originally defined in the HTML file, and for various multimedia operations such as retrieving images and audio files. Note that you do not have complete freedom to resize the applet window, since it has to fit within a maximum space defined by the `<APPLET>` tag in the HTML file. See the `Applet` class in the API for full details of these methods.

2.4 An applet example

In this subsection, we look at a more substantial example of an applet to illustrate the use of some of the methods discussed above.

Activity 10.1
Playing 'Spot the Robot'.

See Subsection 2.7 for a discussion of variations between browsers in how they support applets.

This example is a simple game we call 'Spot the Robot'. This involves a 'magic robot' that can disappear and reappear on the screen in any position. The game requires the user to click, using the mouse, to indicate the position where they think the magic robot will next appear.

For this example, we use an applet class, `SpotTheRobot`, which extends the `Applet` class, rather than the `JApplet` class that we used in the previous example. This should allow the applet to run on a wider variety of browsers. We do not require any of the more advanced features offered by `JApplet`, such as the Swing libraries, so there is no disadvantage in doing this.

Figure 5 contains a typical view of the applet window as shown by the `appletviewer`.

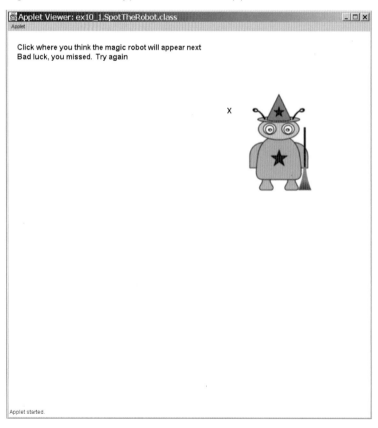

Figure 5   The **SpotTheRobot** applet window as shown by the **appletviewer**

The code for the applet is as follows:

```java
import java.awt.*;
import java.awt.event.*;
import java.applet.*;
import java.util.*;
import java.net.*;

public class SpotTheRobot extends Applet
{
    private Image magicRobotImage;

    private final int WINDOW_X_SIZE = 800;
    private final int WINDOW_Y_SIZE = 800;
    private Font messageFont;
    private Random random;

    private int mouseXPosition;
    private int mouseYPosition;

    private boolean starting;
    // initialize the applet
    public void init ()
    {
        /* Load the magic robot image. Assume that
           the HTML file for this applet is stored in
           the project base folder and that the image is
           stored in subfolder 'images' of this base folder.*/
        magicRobotImage =
            getImage (getCodeBase (), "images/MagicRobot.jpg");

        resize (WINDOW_X_SIZE, WINDOW_Y_SIZE);
        messageFont = new Font ("Sanserif", Font.BOLD, 16);
        random = new Random ();

        this.addMouseListener (new MouseTrap ());
        mouseXPosition = 0;
        mouseYPosition = 0;
    } // end init

    public void start ()
    {
        starting = true; // indicates starting or re-starting
    }

    public void paint (Graphics g)
    {
        g.setFont (messageFont);
        g.drawString ("Click where you think the magic robot will appear next", 20, 40);

        // just display opening message first time
        if (starting)
        {
            starting = false;
        }
```

```
                else // not the first time, so display robot and mouse click
                {
                    int robotWidth = magicRobotImage.getWidth(this);
                    int robotHeight = magicRobotImage.getHeight(this);
                    // choose a random position for the robot
                    int robotXPosition = random.nextInt(WINDOW_X_SIZE - robotWidth);
                    int robotYPosition = random.nextInt(WINDOW_Y_SIZE - robotHeight);

                    // display the robot
                    g.drawImage(magicRobotImage, robotXPosition, robotYPosition,
                                robotWidth, robotHeight, null);

                    // show where the mouse was when last clicked
                    g.drawString("X", mouseXPosition, mouseYPosition);

                // check whether the user clicked in the right place
                Rectangle imageRectangle = new Rectangle(robotXPosition,
                    robotYPosition, robotWidth, robotHeight);
                if (imageRectangle.contains(mouseXPosition, mouseYPosition))
                {
                    g.drawString("Well done, you found the magic robot!", 20, 80);
                    starting = true; // restart the game
                }
                else
                {
                    g.drawString("Bad luck, you missed. Try again", 20, 60);
                }
            }
        }
    } // end paint

    // inner class – keeps track of position of mouse clicks
        class MouseTrap extends MouseAdapter
    {
        // see later for coding details
    } // end MouseTrap
}
```

This applet makes use of two of the four life cycle methods, namely `init` and `start`. It also uses several of the methods listed in Table 2 – it overrides the `paint` method to draw the applet window and also invokes the `getImage` and `resize` methods.

See Subsection 2.5 for the security restrictions on applets.

The `init` method loads the robot image to be used, by invoking the `getImage` method. A special feature of the `getImage` method is that it returns immediately, and the next statement in the `init` method is executed without waiting for the image to complete loading. This is because, in general, the applet would expect to load an image over the web from the server where it originated and this might take a considerable time. The image must be completely loaded before any attempt to display it and the `drawImage` method used later will wait, if necessary, until the image has been loaded.

The applet method `getDocumentBase` returns the URL where the HTML file associated with this applet can be found. This allows it to find the robot image file for the applet.

The `init` method deals with other initialization such as setting the applet window size, the font to be used for displayed messages, and the default values of instance variables.

It also sets up the *random number generating object* and defines a listener to monitor any mouse clicks. This listener is an object of the `MouseTrap` class, which is defined as an inner class of the applet, and is explained in more detail later.

The `paint` method contains most of the code that makes the applet work. This is invoked each time the applet window needs to be redrawn, in particular, after each mouse click made by the user. Using the `Graphics` object referred to by the argument `g`, it invokes the `drawString` and `drawImage` methods of the `Graphics` class to display the current position of the magic robot and the user's guessed position indicated by their mouse click (shown as an 'X'). If the user clicked inside the rectangle that includes the robot image, then a suitable message is displayed. We use the `getWidth` and `getHeight` methods of the `Image` class to find the size of the robot image. We do not do this in the `init` method because, as noted earlier, the image may not have finished loading, and the loading of the image may only be completed after the first attempt to display it.

When the `paint` method for this applet is first invoked, it only displays the message inviting the user to guess. On subsequent invocations, it displays both the user's guess and the position of the robot until the user finds the robot. After a successful guess, it starts the game again. This behaviour is controlled by the `boolean` instance variable `starting`. The `start` method sets the value of this variable to ensure that the applet behaves as if starting, both the first time it is viewed and on any subsequent return to viewing the applet.

Finally, the detailed code for the inner class `MouseTrap` is as follows:

```
// inner class – keeps track of position of mouse clicks
class MouseTrap extends MouseAdapter
{
    // record position of mouse click and redraw the applet
    public void mouseClicked (MouseEvent e)
    {
        mouseXPosition = e.getX();
        mouseYPosition = e.getY();
        repaint(); // invoke the applet paint method
    }
} // end MouseTrap
```

The `MouseTrap` class extends the adapter class `MouseAdapter`, using an approach to event handling discussed in *Unit 7*. The method `mouseClicked` is invoked each time the user presses the mouse button. This records the `x` and `y` positions of the mouse pointer in the instance variables `mouseXPosition` and `mouseYPosition`. The method then invokes the `repaint` method for the applet, which causes the `paint` method to be invoked. This ensures that the positions of the mouse click and of the robot are shown on screen. Figure 6 shows the result of a successful guess.

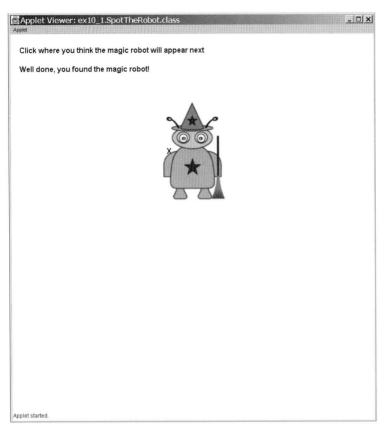

Figure 6   The **SpotTheRobot** applet window after a successful guess

In Figure 6, the X that indicates the position of the user's guess is not exactly on the robot picture, yet it is regarded as a successful guess. This is because we have used a simple algorithm that just checks whether the mouse click is within the bounding rectangle of the image.

The paint method should not normally be invoked directly by your program code – you should use the repaint method, which will, in turn, invoke the paint method, but ensures that other details like the background and foreground colours are correctly set.

An alternative approach to using an inner class like MouseTrap would be to make the applet class itself the listener. To do this, we would declare SpotTheRobot as implementing the MouseListener interface and would then have to provide implementations for all the methods of that interface.

Activity 10.2
Programming an applet.

A 'sandbox' is an American term for a children's sandy playing area.

2.5   The security restrictions on applets

Earlier, we mentioned that there are some restrictions on what applets are normally allowed to do. When these restrictions are in place, the applet is said to be running in the **sandbox**. This is necessary because applets are downloaded and run from web servers, which may be remote and of unknown trustworthiness, perhaps even by accidentally clicking on a web link. It is usually not possible for the user to prevent an applet from running. If applets had no security restrictions, then a badly written or deliberately malicious applet could do enormous damage on the computer that runs the applet.

The standard restrictions that apply to applets are as follows:

▶   they cannot read from or write to the local computer's file system;

▶   they cannot run any other executable programs on the local computer;

▶ they cannot communicate with any computer other than the server from which the applet was downloaded – this is sometimes explained as 'applets can only phone home';

▶ they can only find out very limited information about the local computer, such as the version of Java or the operating system in use;

▶ if an applet creates a pop-up window, the window displays a special warning message.

These restrictions can be enforced because the applet is run by the browser, and the code executed by the applet is monitored by software known as the Java security manager. It is possible to allow applets more freedom, typically when the applet comes from a known and trusted source, such as an intranet. This lifting of some or all security restrictions is done by a process known as signing the applet – this uses cryptography to identify the origin of the applet. The details of **signed applets** and security policies are outside the scope of this unit.

2.6 | When to use applets

In the introduction to this section we explained that, for a period after the first introduction of Java, applets caused great excitement and they were used for many purposes. These included data validation, drawing graphics and animations on web pages as well as carrying out processing of data. As Java technology and other web technologies have developed, Java has become more important as a standard programming language for applications, and applets have become just one of a number of ways to implement more interactive web-based systems. There are now alternative technologies for many of the original uses of applets.

For example, data validation (such as checking the format of numbers entered into forms on the web) is now commonly done using the JavaScript scripting language. JavaScript is a relatively simple language that uses some syntax similar to Java, but is not fully object oriented. Animation often uses animated GIF files (a series of related picture files, which works like an animated cartoon or a simple flip-book) or specialized graphics and animation software that does not require Java programming. Serious processing of data is normally delegated to code running on the server, as server code has none of the security limitations imposed on applets – running complex processing code on the client, possibly by means of an applet, may slow down the client unacceptably and make the user interface seem unresponsive.

However, applets still have many uses. We can identify some characteristics of applets, which help to determine the situations in which applets are appropriate, as follows.

▶ Applets can potentially use the full Java language, which is much more versatile and flexible than many of the alternatives, such as JavaScript.

▶ Applet code can be easily and automatically downloaded along with a web page, even by non-expert users.

▶ Applets run on the client, so they can load the client and relieve the server of work; they can respond quickly to user input at the client.

▶ Standard applets have security restrictions, as we have seen, which limit what they can do directly.

▶ Applets run in a browser, an environment that is available on most computers. There are, however, differences between browsers and version of browsers in how they handle applets or even whether they handle them at all.

From this list, we can see that the key advantages of an applet are that it can be versatile and responsive and can be run easily by non-experts. For this reason, many simple games available on the web are implemented as applets. Typically, these games may need quite sophisticated graphics but are not much concerned with storing data, so the applet security restrictions are not much of a problem.

Another key advantage is the ability to easily download an applet from the web and run it. This means that it is easy to ensure that users access the latest version of software coded in an applet, since they must download the applet code each time they want to use it. Users need not even be aware that they are using an updated version, unless this affects the way they use the system. Compare this with software installed as an application on each client computer, where there will normally be a more complex installation or updating process for new versions.

Because of the diversity of browsers and their behaviour when presented with an applet, it may be that applets with a serious purpose are best limited to operating on intranets or among restricted groups of users, where the behaviour of the browsers can be predicted. If the distribution is to be more widespread, the programmer of the applet must provide for this diversity of browser behaviour, and must carry out testing to ensure that the applet works on a wide range of browsers. Signed applets can be used to relax some of the standard security restrictions, where appropriate.

2.7 Problems with browsers

We have seen that one of the potential advantages of applets is that they run in a browser, an environment that is widely available. This can also be a disadvantage – there are many different browsers and quite a number of versions of the more popular browsers and they vary in their treatment of applets. The browser's Java Virtual Machine (JVM) has historically been provided as part of the browser, without any strong standardization.

Browser versions and browser wars

Very early browsers (pre-dating Java) did not support applets at all. In the early days of Java, the popular browsers supported the early versions of the language such as Java 1.1, but with variations in support for some detailed aspects, and with some vendors implementing their own extensions to the Java language itself.

To make matters worse, there then followed a considerable period of intense competition, sometimes known as the 'browser wars', between the leading browser providers. This had adverse effects on browser compatibility with applets, in that each provider tended to frequently update their browser offerings, adding proprietary features but usually also introducing new bugs along the way. Various legal disputes, other disagreements and the continual turmoil of the competitive market meant that not all browsers kept up with developments in the Java language.

Many current browsers have built-in Java support based on the JDK 1.1 Java platform and, therefore, are not capable of running applets that make use of features added to the Java platform since JDK 1.1. The supported features include the AWT but may not include such fundamental parts of the current language as the Swing user interface library. Therefore, most browsers will support applets based on the `Applet` class, but not necessarily applets that extend the `JApplet` class.

Peace at last?

Fortunately, there is a way out of the unsatisfactory situation described above. Sun Microsystems offers freely downloadable software that can be 'plugged in' to most browsers to enable them to run applets using current versions of Java. The Java Plug-in, as it is called, provides a standard and up-to-date JVM and run-time environment. Effectively, Sun has solved the compatibility problems by taking back control of the browser JVM.

Some systems may come with the Java Plug-in already installed. It is a significant download, but the large download should only be required once, with possible occasional updates when you wish to take advantage of a new version of the Java language. On some platforms the Java Plug-in may be automatically installed when either the Java Runtime Environment or the Java 2 SDK is installed.

If you experience any problems in running applets from a browser, it may be useful to check whether the Java Plug-in is already installed on your computer. The details of how to do this vary between platforms but are readily available on the web.

SAQ 1

(a) Why are applets commonly used for simple games available on the web?

(b) What problems may arise when we try to use such applets?

ANSWERS ....

(a) Simple games can take advantage of the strengths of applets. They are responsive (because they run on the client) and versatile (using the full Java language). Applets can display images and play audio files. Some of the potential limitations of applets are not such a problem – for example, simple games typically do not require much storage and so are not affected by the lack of access to the local file system.

(b) Browsers differ in their support for applets. It may be necessary to load the Java Plug-in before some applets can be successfully run.

3 MIDlets

So far in this course you have made use of the powerful facilities provided by the J2SE edition of Java. In a later section of this unit, you will briefly encounter the J2EE edition of Java, which offers even more powerful features than J2SE. The downside to the functionality and power of these editions of Java are that they make substantial demands for computing resources in terms of memory, processing power and network connectivity to run and make use of them.

However, there are a very large number of computing devices that do not have the memory and processing power of even low specification laptop and desktop computers. Among these are devices such as Personal Digital Assistants (PDAs) and mobile phones. Devices such as these, despite having increasingly powerful processors, memories and full colour screens, still lack the resources needed to run J2SE or J2EE.

The solution to this is a third edition of Java for mobile devices – **J2ME** (Java 2 Micro Edition). J2ME is a collection of API specifications that defines a reduced version of the J2SE platform for a range of small devices such as mobile phones, PDAs and set-top boxes. Applications constructed using J2ME are known as MIDlets. The name comes from applying the diminutive to the acronym for Mobile Information Device. As we shall see, MIDlets are similar to applets and are able to run on small devices.

In this section, we focus on programming for mobile phones. Although primarily used for voice communication, increasingly mobile phones are being supplied as Java enabled devices capable of running Java applications. These applications can range from simple applications, to hold a shopping list, to very sophisticated games. In addition, these Java applications can make use of the inherent connectivity of the devices that they are running on.

While we will not be able to go through the whole of the development and publishing life cycle of an application, this section will show how you can use the knowledge of Java that you have developed so far to write programs that will run on mobile phone sized devices. You have been supplied with a toolkit that provides mobile phone emulators on which you will be able to try out your applications. At the end of this section, we will briefly look at issues surrounding the porting of applications to mobile devices.

The J2ME technology encompasses almost (if not more in many ways) as wide a range of issues and features as does the J2SE technology. This section will only be able to give you a flavour of the scope and potential of the J2ME technology, but it should allow you to then follow the detailed APIs with confidence. We will give you the core skills and knowledge needed to explore the fascinating and booming area of computing for mobile devices. This is a quickly developing area of IT and mobile (abbreviated 'm') applications are already plentiful, with fields such as m-gaming, m-commerce and m-learning making use of increasingly powerful devices and new API specifications.

In order to run any of the examples in this section, you will need to use the Wireless Toolkit and its Java Environment. Activity 3 shows you a number of demonstration MIDlets to illustrate their range and sophistication.

Activity 10.3
Running a MIDlet example.

3.1 | Configurations and profiles

Unlike J2SE, J2ME is not a single specification but rather a collection of specifications. This is a response to the very wide range of devices available, each with very different capabilities in terms of memory, functionality, speed, network access, and so on. As a result of this range of capabilities, it is not possible to specify a single environment to cover all of these devices while making best use of the functionality of all of them.

J2ME currently defines two basic configurations based on the memory, processing speed and network connectivity that are available on target devices. Each of these configurations defines a core set of class libraries along with a virtual machine on which they will run. These are as follows.

Connected Limited Device Configuration (**CLDC**) is aimed at small resource devices such as mobile phones. This configuration is designed for devices with intermittent network connections and because of the limited resources available, the class libraries run on an abridged version of the Java Virtual Machine called the Kilobyte Virtual Machine (KVM). Typically, this configuration is aimed at devices with 128Kb to 512Kb of memory.

Connected Device Configuration (**CDC**) is aimed at higher specification devices such as PDAs and set-top boxes. This configuration uses JVM and has a wider range of APIs available. We will not consider CDC any further in this course.

Configurations, however, are only part of the story. Even within each configuration there is a huge range of devices and so we have profiles to target particular categories of device and particular applications. Each profile has APIs additional to those in the configurations. The profile that we will focus on in this course is the Mobile Information Device Profile (**MIDP**). This is designed for mobile phones and provides APIs for user interfaces and network connectivity suitable for these devices. MIDP requires these devices to have a minimum display of 96 pixels by 54 pixels and to support at least two colours. Of course, many devices currently being used have displays far superior to this specification and it is one of the tasks of the MIDlet programmer to ensure that they either design their MIDlet for a specific device or make use of the various language features that allow a MIDlet to interrogate the device that it is running on.

There are many optional packages currently available or specified that are aimed at particular tasks and devices, such as Java APIs for Bluetooth, Mobile 3D Graphics, Games, Security and Trust.

So, for any particular device, there is a combination of a configuration and at least one profile, which provides a complete run-time environment.

Figure 7 shows an overview of the relationship between the CLDC and profiles for mobile phones.

A number of mobile phone companies provide APIs specific to their own range of phones. An example can be seen at http://www.forum.nokia. com for Nokia.

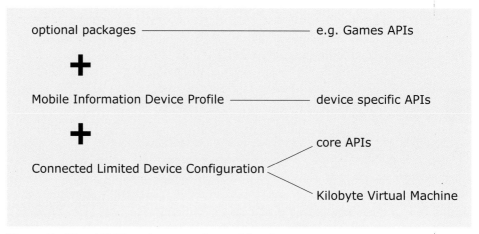

Figure 7   The J2ME environment for mobile phones

Java applications that run within the CLDC–MIDP environment are known as MIDlets. When you use an application such as a game on a mobile phone, it is a MIDlet that is running on the virtual machine embedded within the phone. Many applications are single MIDlets and we will be looking at these applications in this section. However, some applications are made up of a suite of MIDlets. These tend to be more sophisticated applications and MIDlets within a suite can share data and resources. In this section we will only consider applications composed of one MIDlet.

3.2   MIDlets

Here is our first look at a MIDlet:

```java
import javax.microedition.midlet.*;
import javax.microedition.lcdui.*;

public class HelloWorld extends MIDlet
{
    private TextBox textbox;
    private Display display;
    private static final int screenLength = 20;

    public HelloWorld ()
    {
    }

    public void startApp ()
    {
        textbox = new TextBox("First MIDlet", "Hello World",
                            screenLength,TextField.ANY);
        display = Display.getDisplay(this);
        display.setCurrent(textbox);
    }

    public void pauseApp ()
    {
    }

    public void destroyApp (boolean b)
    {
    }
}
```

As you can see, there are some new packages to import but essentially the MIDlet has a recognizable structure and, indeed, is similar to the structure of an applet. When the emulator is run with this code we are presented with a screen showing the available MIDlets – only `MyHello` in this case, since this was the project name used (as you will see when you carry out Activity 4). Figure 8 shows this initial screen.

Figure 8   Initial MIDlet screen

Once this MIDlet has been launched by the user selecting the soft-key associated with Launch (this is usually the button below Launch on the emulator phone keypad) then the MIDlet `startApp` method runs and the screen in Figure 9 is displayed.

Figure 9   The running MIDlet

MIDlet structure

Activity 10.4
Writing a MIDlet.

The code for the `HelloWorld` MIDlet shows the main points about the structure of a MIDlet. Typically, a MIDlet inherits from the `MIDlet` class and often implements `CommandListener` as well. We will meet `CommandListener` shortly, but for now we can put it to one side. This particular MIDlet makes use of what is known as a high level user interface where we have access to system-provided components such as `TextBox`, `TextField`, `Gauge` and `List`. We will look more closely at high level user interfaces shortly, as well as low level user interfaces, which provide better support for games functionality.

The class `HelloWorld` contains four methods. One of them is a constructor where routine initialization can take place. If there is no initialization required then the constructor can be omitted (and the system will use the default no argument constructor as with J2SE) or left empty as we have done here. However, the other three methods are required to be present although as you can see they do not need to have any code. They are required to be present because the basic `MIDlet` class is an abstract class and its three methods must be overridden. These three methods move the MIDlet through the various possible states that it can be in. Figure 10 shows these possible states.

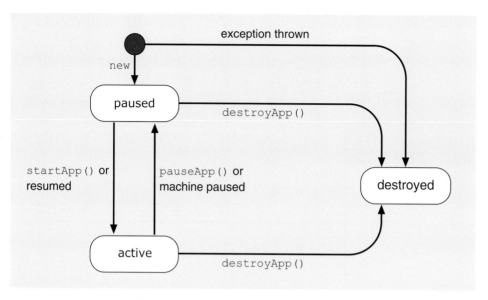

Figure 10   Possible MIDlet states and transitions

When a MIDlet is first constructed it goes into the paused state. From here, it will typically go into the active state by `startApp` being called or by the device resuming the MIDlet after an interruption. The MIDlet can move back into the paused state by either invoking `pauseApp` or by the device pausing the MIDlet itself. In the case of a phone call coming through, the device will pause the MIDlet itself and call the `pauseApp` method.

When programming MIDlets we need to be aware that the device on which they run may often pause them, and so the `pauseApp` method must contain any code needed to save data, stop any timers, and so on.

It is important to realize from the above that the `startApp` and `pauseApp` methods may be invoked many times while the MIDlet is executing, but that the constructor will only be invoked once. So the programmer needs to think carefully where initializations are carried out, and whether some sections of the `startApp` method in particular need to be guarded from running whenever `startApp` is invoked.

From the active state, the MIDlet can also move into the destroyed state where it must release all resources being held. This is done using the `destroyApp` method. The MIDlet can also move into the destroyed state from the paused state on creation if there is a problem constructing the MIDlet.

The `destroyApp` method notifies the application that it is to be destroyed. The parameter `unconditional` is set to true to indicate that the MIDlet must release its resources and that it will definitely move into the destroyed state. However, if the `unconditional` parameter is set to false, it is an indication that the application requests to stay in its current state, that is the paused or active state. If this request can be granted (which will depend on the availability of resources) the method will throw a `MIDletStateChangeException`. To tell the platform that the MIDlet can now be terminated, we invoke the `notifyDestroyed` method.

In summary, the required methods are:

▶ `startApp` – called to put the MIDlet in active state from paused state, if failure occurs then it calls `destroyApp` and throws `MIDletStateChangeException`;

▶ `pauseApp` – called to put the MIDlet into paused state from active state;

▶ `destroyApp` – depending on the value of the parameter `unconditional`, this is either a notification that the MIDlet must release its resources and move to the destroyed state, or it is a request to remain in the current state, and throwing a `MIDletStateChangeException` if the request can be granted.

Decisions as to whether a MIDlet moves from one state to another are taken by the Application Management Software (AMS). This is the environment in which a MIDlet is installed, started and stopped. It is also known as the Java Application Manager (JAM).

Before we look in detail at creating MIDlets, we briefly outline some key Java features that are not available to MIDlets. These features are absent due to either the limited memory available or the processing power needed. The most obvious absentees are that there are no facilities for handling `float` and `double`, and that there are none of the GUI features from the AWT and Swing libraries (although there are reasonable alternatives available). An implication of this is that none of the `Maths` methods using `float`s or `double`s are available. We will also see that there are important differences in network connectivity between J2SE and J2ME and that there is limited exception handling.

There are many other differences and we need to consult the detailed APIs before designing a MIDlet.

3.3 The `Displayable` class

The approach that we will take in our tour of J2ME is to focus on one particular class – the `Displayable` class. This is a key class in producing visible interfaces on mobile devices. Virtually every MIDlet has a user interface and so we will concentrate on producing user interfaces, and then allow you to use your imagination and knowledge to develop interesting applications. The use of MIDlets is developing very rapidly with exciting applications being created all of the time.

A MIDlet can only display a single screen at any particular time. As we will see, the programmer can give the user the opportunity to display another screen but never more than one at a time. The physical screen is represented logically by the `Display` class and each MIDlet has access to only one instance of this class. Most MIDlets will get a reference to the `Display` object in their `startApp` method using the following code:

```
public static Display getDisplay(MIDlet mid);
```

The result of the method call will be assigned to a suitable variable, as any call to `getDisplay` will always return the same value for any given MIDlet. For example:

```
display = Display.getDisplay(this);
```

This variable can now be used within the program to avoid any further calls to `getDisplay`.

Interacting with the screen

There are two useful methods that can be used to set and get the current screen. These are `setCurrent(newInterface)`, where `newInterface` is of type `Displayable`, and `getCurrent()`. Any user interface features that we want to have shown on the screen are held in a container called `Displayable` – this is an abstract class, which when subclassed is able to hold items such as text boxes, text fields and images, and also drawn images as in a game.

The `Displayable` class though is too general to cover the very different needs of data field type interactions and graphical type interactions, and so there are two subclasses of `Displayable`. One is called `Screen` and is used for **high level user interfaces**, and the other is called `Canvas` and is used for **low level user interfaces**. Both these classes are abstract. The subclass, `Screen`, has four concrete subclasses and these are the classes that are generally used. The other subclass is `Canvas`, and a developer can either subclass `Canvas` or use its subclass called `GameCanvas`. We will subclass `Canvas` in order to illustrate some of the key issues to be considered, such as the need to implement a `paint` method. The high level user interface classes are designed to provide components that are portable from one device to another as the detailed implementation in terms of, for example, font size, scrolling and display are taken care of by the particular device. The low level user interface class is less portable and requires the programmer to specify how the subject that is drawn on the screen is displayed and how the user is able to interact with the screen. Figure 11 shows the class hierarchy for the `Displayable` class.

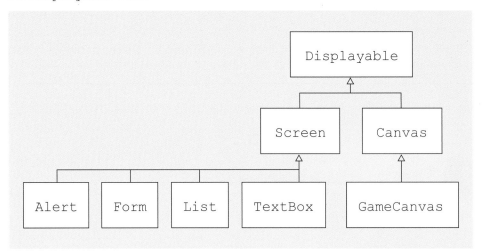

Figure 11   The **Displayable** class hierarchy

We will now consider each of the main subclasses in more detail.

3.4 | High level interfaces

The advantage of using the high level interfaces is that they provide a set of easy-to-use features. The disadvantage is that the developer has little control over how the interface will actually look on any particular mobile phone. Developers will normally use one of the four concrete subclasses of `Screen`. We will concentrate on two of these: the `Form` and the `TextBox` classes. The `Alert`s are used to produce short messages on screen and `List`s offer similar functionality to `List`s in J2SE.

You have already met an example of the use of `TextBox`. This is a simple way to present the user with text either just for them to read or for them to edit and/or use as data input. Rather than go laboriously through a set of options and features of the `TextBox` class through a series of small snippets of code, we will make use of the Java knowledge that you have gained so far and look at some of the key features of a longer complete program.

TextBox

When selected, the MIDlet below will display a text box on the screen and will invite users to delete the text present (either using the CLEAR button on the phone or selecting the CLEAR option on the menu using the multidirectional keys and the SELECT central key) and 'type in' via the keyboard on this emulation or by using the standard 'SMS texting' approach, their own text. When users select the GO option from the menu, their text will appear as a moving 'ticker' on the screen, that is, an area of continuously scrolling text. The text on the ticker can be changed as often as the user wishes. The user is also able to stop the MIDlet at any time by pressing the key associated with the STOP command.

```
import javax.microedition.midlet.*;
import javax.microedition.lcdui.*;
```

```java
public class TextBoxExample extends MIDlet implements CommandListener
{
    private TextBox textbox;
    private Display display;
    private static final int screenLength = 100;

    // commands
    private static final Command STOP = new Command("Stop", Command.EXIT, 0);
    private static final Command CLEAR = new Command("Clear Screen", Command.SCREEN, 1);
    private static final Command GO = new Command("GO", Command.SCREEN, 1);


    public TextBoxExample ()
    {
    }

    public void startApp ()
    {
        textbox = new TextBox("TextBoxExample", "Delete this text and enter your own,
                        then select option GO", screenLength, TextField.ANY);

        // add commands
        textbox.addCommand(STOP);
        textbox.addCommand(CLEAR);
        textbox.addCommand(GO);
        textbox.setCommandListener(this);

        // display the screen
        display = Display.getDisplay(this);
        display.setCurrent(textbox);
    }
    public void pauseApp ()
    {
    }

    public void destroyApp (boolean b)
    {
    }

    // command Actions
    public void commandAction (Command c, Displayable d)
    {
        if (c == GO)
        {
            String text = textbox.getString();
            // create the Ticker
            Ticker ticker = new Ticker(text);
            textbox.setTicker(ticker);
        }
        if (c == STOP)
        {
            destroyApp(true);
            notifyDestroyed();
        }
```

```
        if (c == CLEAR)
        {
            textbox.setString(null);
        }
    }
}
```

When selected, the above MIDlet presents the user with an initial screen as shown in Figure 12.

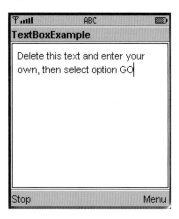

Figure 12   Initial screen for **TextBoxExample** MIDlet

Once the screen has been cleared and new text entered, then selecting the GO option from the menu will give a ticker display as shown in Figure 13.

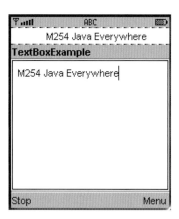

Figure 13   Ticker display with entered text

This MIDlet still has a very simple structure. The class `TextBoxExample` extends `MIDlet` as before and now implements `CommandListener`, this will allow the user to interact with the MIDlet. We shall explain the details of this in a moment.

The general structure is as follows: variable and final declarations (three of which are to do with user interactions), an empty constructor (which could be omitted), then the three standard methods of a MIDlet – `startApp`, `pauseApp` and `destroyApp` – and then the `commandAction` method.

Once again, the main code is in the `startApp` method.

The line

```
textbox = new TextBox("TextBoxExample","Delete this text and enter
                      your own, then select option GO", screenLength,
                      TextField.ANY);
```

instantiates a `TextBox` with the title `TextBoxExample` and with initial contents `"Delete this text ... option GO"`. The variable `screenLength` determines the maximum number of characters that the text box can hold. A value has to be given and if set to a value greater than the actual screen can hold, then the user will be given the facility to scroll up and down the screen in some device-dependent way – usually by means of the multidirectional key. This value determines the maximum number of characters that the user can enter and anything in excess of this will be ignored. The final argument allows any form of text to be entered. Constraints can be placed on the type of input allowed and data will be checked by the system to ensure it fits the given pattern. For example, `TextField.NUMERIC` restricts the input to numbers.

The final two lines of `startApp` display the text box as has been explained before:

```
display = Display.getDisplay(this);
display.setCurrent(textbox);
```

With this code, we have a text box that will be displayed on screen and with which users can interact – they can add text (up to a maximum of 100 characters) and they can delete text. However, nothing will happen beyond this. We need to give users the ability to cause code to run as a result of the changes that they have made. To do this, we need to look at handling commands.

Adding interaction

The treatment of commands in J2ME is quite similar to the treatment of events in J2SE.

▶ A command (rather than event) listener class is written, which defines some behaviour to be executed if the user activates a particular command.

▶ A listener object is created and registered with the relevant display object.

▶ When the system detects that the user has activated the command, the appropriate method, such as `commandAction`, is automatically invoked on the listener object.

One difference is that in J2ME we define the range of commands available to the user, whereas in the AWT event model the possible events are predefined. When a method such as `commandAction` is invoked, the command is passed as an argument and used to determine what action is to be taken.

In order to use a command listener, we proceed as follows.

Step 1   Defining the command options

To start we need to define the command options that we wish the user to have. The display of these command options is device dependent but there is some limited scope for the developer to influence the display.

In the example, we have three commands, `STOP`, `CLEAR` and `GO`. To define `STOP`, for instance, we use the statement:

```
private static final Command STOP =
    new Command("Stop", Command.EXIT, 0);
```

Mobile devices usually do not have sufficient screen space to display buttons and menu bars for individual options, and so the device will make decisions as to how the options are to be presented to the user.

The `Command` constructor has the following three arguments.

▶ The first argument gives the command a label, which the device will attempt to display in some way.

▶ The second argument gives the type of the command.

▶ The third argument sets the priority. This allows the developer to indicate to the device the relative importance of the command.

To see how the priority is used, consider a mobile phone. Typically, this will have two 'soft buttons', one placed underneath the right-hand side of the screen and the other under the left-hand side of the screen. These buttons then respond to the command displayed on the screen directly above them.

If there are more than two commands – as in our example – then on a mobile phone, each command cannot be allocated its own soft key. In that case, the system running on the device will have to make a decision on how the commands will be displayed.

You can see the outcome of such a decision in Figure 12. On the left-hand side we have `Stop` and on the right-hand side `Menu`. Three commands were too many for the device to display with two soft keys, and so two were placed in a menu and the other was displayed on the left-hand side.

In general, the effect of a priority value is that the lower it is, the more likely a command is to get a soft key of its own. However, the outcome is also dependent on the type of command; command types such as `Command.EXIT` and `Command.BACK` tend to be favoured over more general commands such as `Command.SCREEN`. This is the reason why in our example `STOP`, of type `EXIT`, was assigned its own soft key.

Step 2   Adding commands to a `Displayable` object

To add the commands to the text box we use the `addCommand` method. In our example, the commands are added by the three statements:

```
textbox.addCommand(STOP);
textbox.addCommand(CLEAR);
textbox.addCommand(GO);
```

Step 3   Registering a `CommandListener` with the relevant `Displayable` object

In our example, we need to register a `CommandListener` to a `TextBox`. This is done by invoking the `setCommandListener` method.

Step 4   Defining a `CommandListener` class

We need to define a class that will implement the `CommandListener` interface, but override the `commandAction` method to provide the required behaviour. Method `commandAction` is passed two parameters: one is the command invoked by the user and the other is a reference to the displayable interface with which it is associated. With the aid of this information it can update the interface to reflect the result of the user's action.

In our example, we have declared our MIDlet as implementing `commandListener` and so made it possible for the MIDlet itself to be registered as a listener of the objects in its own display. This is a very common technique, also often used with applets and other GUI displays.

Since the MIDlet implements `commandListener` it must implement the `commandAction` method that belongs to that interface, as follows:

```
public void commandAction (Command c, Displayable d)
{
    if (c == GO)
    {
        String text = textbox.getString();
        // create the Ticker
        Ticker ticker = new Ticker(text);
        textbox.setTicker(ticker);
    }
    if (c == STOP)
```

```
    {
        destroyApp(true);
        notifyDestroyed();
    }
    if (c == CLEAR)
    {
        textbox.setString(null);
    }
}
```

From this, it should be fairly clear what effect it has.

▶   GO gets the current contents of the text box and instantiates and installs a ticker on the text box.

▶   STOP invokes the destroyApp method, which arranges for a safe termination of resources and then notifyDestroyed tells the platform that this MIDlet can be terminated.

▶   CLEAR sets the text box to the null string.

The ticker can be seen in Figure 13, at the top of the screen and above the text box label. The placing and scrolling speed of a ticker is system dependent.

Form

The second subclass of Screen that we will look at is the Form class. This class provides an easy way to construct user interfaces from a collection of items, such as TextField, StringItem and Gauges (a gauge is in effect a progress bar, however, the actual representation of it is device dependent). Commands can also be associated with these interfaces as they were with TextBox. All Items are subclasses of the abstract class Item. The class Form has the following two constructors, the first creates an empty Form with a title and the second creates a Form with a title and a set of Items held in an array.

```
public Form(String title);
public Form(String title, Item [] items);
```

Items can be added to a Form using one of three append methods:

```
public void append(Item item);
public void append(Image image);
public void append(String string);
```

Again, we will use an illustrative MIDlet to focus on some key features of the Form and Item classes. The following MIDlet uses a Form to display a text field to users inviting them to enter some text up to a total of 20 characters. As the text is entered, the gauge below the text field indicates how much of the text field space has been used. This simple program is used to demonstrate an alternative form of interaction with a Screen object using the ItemStateListener interface.

```
import javax.microedition.midlet.*;
import javax.microedition.lcdui.*;

public class FormExample extends MIDlet implements ItemStateListener
{
    private Form form;
    private Display display;
    private TextField textfield;
    private Gauge gauge;
```

```java
    public FormExample ()
    {
    }

    public void startApp ()
    {
        form = new Form ("FormExample");

        // create Text Field and add to Form
        textfield = new TextField("Input some number of characters
                                up to 20", null, 20,
                                TextField.ANY);
        form.append(textfield);
        // create Gauge and add to Form
        gauge = new Gauge ("Number of characters input", false, 20, 0);
        form.append(gauge);

        // add ItemStateListener
        form.setItemStateListener(this);

        // display form
        display = Display.getDisplay(this);
        display.setCurrent(form);
    }

    public void pauseApp ()
    {
    }

    public void destroyApp (boolean b)
    {
    }

    // add code when text field changes
    public void itemStateChanged (Item it)
    {
        if (it instanceof TextField)
        {
            int number = textfield.getString().length();
            gauge.setValue(number);
        }
    }
}
```

Figure 14 shows the result of the above program.

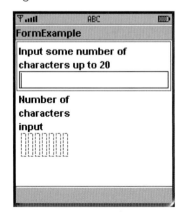

Figure 14   The initial screen for **FormExample**

After some text has been added the screen, as shown in Figure 15, is visible.

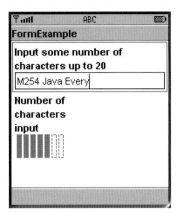

Figure 15   **FormExample** after text has been entered

This program makes use of the `ItemStateListener`, which is similar to the `CommandListener` (which can also be used on `Forms`) that we met earlier. As its name suggests, it listens for changes in the state of any of the `Items` appended to a `Form`. The major difference between the two types of listeners is that the `ItemStateListener` will respond as soon as a change is detected and will not wait for a command option to be selected by the user. This type of response can be more useful for some types of interfaces.

The listener is registered with the MIDlet as follows:

```
form.setItemStateListener(this);
```

and it has one method which has to be implemented:

```
public void itemStateChanged(Item it)
{
    if (it instanceof TextField)
    {
        int number = textfield.getString().length();
        gauge.setValue(number);
    }
}
```

In this case, we are only looking at state changes to one of the items – the `TextField`. If the item that has changed is an instance of a `TextField` then the current length of the string in the field is found and the gauge is updated. The response time for detecting a state change is device dependent and so may not respond as quickly as you might like.

The gauge itself is created by:

```
gauge = new Gauge("Number of characters input", false, 20, 0);
```

The initial string acts as a label, `false` says that the user cannot interact directly with the gauge, 20 is the maximum value and 0 is the initial value of the gauge. There is no developer control over how the gauge will be displayed; this is entirely device dependent.

Resource files

A final `Item` that we will look at is the `StringItem` and we will use it to introduce you to the resource folder to hold files that can be read by a MIDlet. This means that you do not need to include text files within the program code, for example, and these can also be changed more easily than if they were in the MIDlet code itself. Resource files should be placed in the `res/` folder. These files can then be accessed by a running MIDlet. The `StringItem` is the simplest `Item` and provides a means of placing a string with an associated label onto a `Form`.

The MIDlet below displays a Form that holds a single Item – a StringItem. The contents of the StringItem are obtained from a text file in the res/ folder.

```java
import javax.microedition.midlet.*;
import javax.microedition.lcdui.*;
import java.io.*;
import java.lang.String;

public class Resources extends MIDlet
{
    private Form form;
    private Display display;
    private String string;
    private StringItem str;

    public Resources ()
    {
    }

    public void startApp ()
    {
        form = new Form("Resources");
        string = null;
        try
        {
            // access the resources folder
            InputStream is = form.getClass().getResourceAsStream
            ("/res/text1.txt");
            InputStreamReader ir = new InputStreamReader(is);

            // create buffer
            char[] buffer = new char[100];
            StringBuffer sb = new StringBuffer();
            int count = 0;

            // read in characters one by one
            while ((count = ir.read(buffer, 0, buffer.length)) > -1)
            {
                sb.append(buffer, 0, count);
            }
            string = sb.toString();

            // convert to StringItem and append to form
            str = new StringItem(null, string);
            form.append(str);
        }
        catch (IOException ex)
        {
            str = new StringItem(null, "empty");
            form.append(str);
        }

        // display form
        display = Display.getDisplay(this);
        display.setCurrent(form);
    }
```

```
    public void pauseApp ()
    {
    }

    public void destroyApp (boolean b)
    {
    }
}
```

The link to the contents of the `res/` folder is made in the following line:

```
    InputStream is = form.getClass().getResourceAsStream("/res/text1.txt");
```

An `InputStream` is obtained by invoking the `getResourcesAsStream` method. This method takes a `String` holding an absolute pathway to the particular resource – in this case, a text file called `text1` which the system expects to find in the `res/` folder. The `getResouceAsStream` method has to be invoked on a class and `form.getClass` returns the class of the `Form` in the MIDlet. A loop is then used to put the characters of the file into a `StringBuffer`. The commonly used (in J2SE) `BufferedReader` class is not available in J2ME. The `StringItem` itself is produced by:

```
    str = new StringItem(null, string);
```

A `StringItem` has two arguments. The first is a `string` that acts as a label that will precede the second `string`. In this case `null` indicates that there will be no label to this `StringItem`. The value of `string` is then put into the `StringItem`, which is then appended to the `Form` object and then displayed. Figure 16 illustrates the result.

Figure 16 **StringItem** using files stored in the resources folder

This brings us to the end of our tour of high level interfaces. We have seen two types of graphical user interface – the `TextBox` and the `Form`, and we have seen two kinds of interaction – `CommandListener` and `ItemStateListener`. We have also seen a number of `Items` that can be used on a `Form` to produce interfaces easily.

We will now look at low level interfaces where the developer has complete control over the visible screen.

Activity 10.5
Using high level interfaces.

3.5 Low level interfaces

As with the high level interfaces, the low level interfaces have advantages and disadvantages. The main advantage is that the developer has complete control of most of the device screen. The main disadvantage is that the developer has to program all aspects of the interface.

The area of the display device under the control of the developer is that between the signal strength and the battery icon at the top and the command area at the bottom. Some device manufacturers provide additional APIs that allow the developer to make use of the whole device display screen, which is particularly useful for applications such as games.

We will start by looking at the `Canvas` class and show how simple graphical images can be produced on screen before we go on to look at how to deal with event handling.

Canvas

Low level interfaces are based on the `Canvas` class, which we met earlier – it is an abstract subclass of `Displayable`. So when we make use of `Canvas` we have to extend it and implement the `paint` method, which acts in the same way as in J2SE. Also, as with J2SE, we do not invoke `paint` directly but instead invoke `repaint`. The class `Canvas` also has a number of concrete methods that allow the MIDlet to find out about the physical nature of the display device on which it is running. We will focus on two of these methods:

```
public int getWidth()
```

which returns the screen width in pixels and

```
public int getHeight()
```

which returns the screen height in pixels. Other methods are available that can determine whether the display supports colour, pointing devices, and so on.

Most of the techniques and ideas that you met in *Unit 6* and *Unit 7* on AWT and Swing are directly applicable to MIDlets. Many of the same drawing methods are available.

As an example of using low level interfaces we will look at a simple MIDlet in which a circle is drawn on the screen and then by using the multidirectional arrow keys, the circle can be moved around the screen. The MIDlet is composed of two classes. The first one, `SimpleGraphics`, has the basic MIDlet structure and creates an instance of `MyCanvas` and makes use of the constructor to show that to a large extent much code can go into either the constructor or the `startApp` method. The `startApp` method then uses the instance of `MyCanvas` as the current screen to be displayed.

```
import javax.microedition.midlet.*;
import javax.microedition.lcdui.*;

public class SimpleGraphics extends MIDlet
{
    private Display display;
    private MyCanvas canvas;
    public SimpleGraphics ()
    {
        display = Display.getDisplay(this);
        canvas = new MyCanvas();
    }
```

```
        public void startApp ()
        {
            display.setCurrent(canvas);
        }
        public void pauseApp ()
        {
        }

        public void destroyApp (boolean b)
        {
        }
    }
```

The functionality of the MIDlet resides largely in the `MyCanvas` class.

```
import javax.microedition.midlet.*;
import javax.microedition.lcdui.*;

public class MyCanvas extends Canvas
{
    private int width, height, widthPosition, heightPosition;

    public MyCanvas ()
    {
        width = getWidth();
        height = getHeight();
        widthPosition = width/3;
        heightPosition = height/3;
    }

    public void paint (Graphics g)
    {
        // clear screen
        g.setColor(0xffffff);
        g.fillRect(0, 0, width, height);

        // draw circle
        g.setColor(0);
        g.drawArc(widthPosition, heightPosition, width/4, height/4,
                0, 360);
    }

    protected void keyPressed (int keyCode)
    {
        if (getGameAction(keyCode) == Canvas.UP)
        {
            heightPosition = heightPosition - 1;
            repaint();
        }
        if (getGameAction(keyCode) == Canvas.DOWN)
        {
            heightPosition = heightPosition + 1;
            repaint();
        }
```

```
if (getGameAction(keyCode) == Canvas.LEFT)
{
    widthPosition = widthPosition - 1;
    repaint();
}
if (getGameAction(keyCode) == Canvas.RIGHT)
{
    widthPosition = widthPosition + 1;
    repaint();
}
}
}
```

The structure of this class is the same as that of any standard class in J2SE. We have a constructor handling initializations and we override the `paint` method as we do in J2SE. First, let us consider the `paint` method shown above.

This simple `paint` method clears the screen by filling in a screen-sized rectangle with white. It then draws a circle using the `drawArc` method. This takes six arguments, the first two representing the top left-hand corner of a box within which the circle will be drawn. The next two arguments are the width and height of the arc, which are equal since this is a circle. The final two arguments give the angle in degrees through which the arc should be drawn. In this case, it goes from zero degrees to 360 degrees and so forms a complete circle. Figure 17 shows the initial screen display.

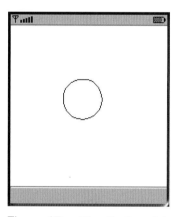

Figure 17   **SimpleGraphics** display

Of more interest is the ability for the user to interact with the graphical display. This is achieved by making use of other methods from the `Canvas` class. Due to the wide range of devices a MIDlet might run on, a developer is quite limited in the keys that can be assumed to be present on a mobile phone. The only keys that are guaranteed to be present are the numbers 0 to 9, the # and * keys. Each of these is assigned a standard key code. However, on our emulator we have a multidirectional key as well and we have made use of this here.

Below is the `keyPressed` method. This method registers when a user has pressed a key. There are two other similar methods:

```
protected void keyReleased (int keyCode);
```

and

```
protected void keyRepeated (int keyCode);
```

The method `keyPressed` is invoked when the user presses a key. To determine which key has been pressed, we use another method from the `Canvas` class called `getGameAction`. This converts the key code generated by the key press into one of the actions corresponding to the multidirectional key. Of course, if the device does not have this multidirectional key then there will be no interaction. For devices on which there is a multidirectional key there are standard codes: UP, DOWN, LEFT and RIGHT. These are then used to suitably change the values of heightPosition and widthPosition and then to call repaint to have the circle drawn again with different coordinates from the top left-hand corner of the enclosing box.

```
protected void keyPressed (int keyCode)
{
    if (getGameAction(keyCode) == Canvas.UP)
    {
        heightPosition = heightPosition - 1;
        repaint();
    }

    if (getGameAction(keyCode) == Canvas.DOWN)
    {
        heightPosition = heightPosition + 1;
        repaint();
    }

    if (getGameAction(keyCode) == Canvas.LEFT)
    {
        widthPosition = widthPosition - 1;
        repaint();
    }

    if (getGameAction(keyCode) == Canvas.RIGHT)
    {
        widthPosition = widthPosition + 1;
        repaint();
    }
}
```

After a few key presses a typical screen is as shown in Figure 18.

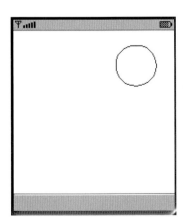

Figure 18   **SimpleGraphics** display after several key presses

There is, of course, a great deal more that can be done graphically. However, we hope that we have given you a flavour of the potential of low level interfaces.

Activity 10.6
Using low level interfaces.

3.6   Persistent storage

MIDlets often need to store and retrieve information. We have seen in one of the examples above how data can be held in the resources folder and then accessed by the running MIDlet. However, sometimes the J2ME equivalent of local file space in J2SE is needed.

The MIDP specification provides for such storage space although how this is actually implemented is device dependent and is unlikely to be disk based. MIDP provides a package called the Record Management System. This contains a class called the `RecordStore`, which is a collection of persistent records. So device memory constraints allowing – a MIDlet is able to store information that is accessible to the MIDlet not only while it is running but also across invocations. The MIDlet is able to access the record store when it is next run. Earlier we mentioned that a MIDlet may be packaged with other MIDlets to form a suite. If one MIDlet in a suite creates a record store, then all of the MIDlets in that suite have access to the record store. However, MIDlets not part of that suite will not be able to access the record store. This is one of the few security features present within MIDP.

The `RecordStore` class has a number of static methods for managing a record store. These include methods for adding, deleting, retrieving and modifying records. There is also a listener, which is able to notify the system about changes to a record store.

A record is a byte array and so can hold a set of arbitrary data. The amount of memory available to a MIDlet is very much device dependent and can range from a few kilobytes to several megabytes.

3.7   Networking MIDlets

Mobile phones (and many other mobile devices such as PDAs) achieve a considerable portion of their usefulness by being able to communicate with the outside world. It would be a distinct advantage therefore if MIDlets could make use of this connectivity.

Such connectivity is provided for by the CLDC configuration and the MIDP specification. The CLDC specification defines an abstract Generic Connection Framework (GCF) which represents all forms of external connections as one of six basic types. The two most important types are stream based connections and datagrams.

However, the CLDC specification does not define any actual implementations of any of the six connection types. This is due to the very broad range of devices that the CLDC specification covers. Instead it is the MIDP specification that provides specific implementations of the GCF. Of the six basic connection types, the MIDP specification only requires devices to implement one of the connection types, the HTTP stream-based connection. Particular devices may implement other connection types but to ensure portability the developer can only assume this one connection type. MIDP does not assume that devices are permanently attached to a network and it doesn't assume TCP/IP is available.

Using only HTTP client connection means that the server is unable to initiate contact with the device except in reply to a request from the client. This connection has the standard HTTP methods, such as GET to request a resource from the server and POST which is used to send information to the server perhaps from a form-based query. Over time it is likely that additional connection types will become more widely available. For the present, the HTTP connection type is most widely used to download MIDlets from websites – this is the topic of the next subsection.

3.8 MIDlet packaging

So far we have concentrated entirely on writing MIDlets that run on an emulator. In the real world, we want to be able to write MIDlets and deploy them so that they can be made available to potentially many devices.

The actual technical details of how to do this are not particularly difficult to understand, but again there is not sufficient space for us to do any more than provide a brief overview of the issues involved.

There are three basic methods of porting a MIDlet from a development environment to an actual mobile device:

▶ factory installation;

▶ direct porting by cable or Infra Red (IR) link;

▶ over-the-air downloading via HTTP using WAP.

In whatever way the MIDlets are transferred, they need to be in a particular format. MIDlets and their resources are held in a file with an extension of .jar. In addition to the **JAR** file which actually holds the MIDlet suite, there are a number of other files that need to be packaged with it. For example, if we are downloading a MIDlet over-the-air, the first thing actually downloaded to the mobile device is a **JAD** (Java Application Descriptor) file. This contains information needed by the mobile device to decide whether it is possible to download the JAR file. Part of the information that must be included in the JAD file is the URL of the JAR file and the JAR file size. If the JAR file can be downloaded, then the AMS (Application Management Software) of the device uses the URL address and downloads the JAR file held at that location. Associated with the JAR file is a Manifest file, which contains information about the profile(s) and the configuration used by the MIDlets and details of the MIDlets enclosed. If everything is satisfactory, then the AMS will install the MIDlets and they are then available for the user to run.

Security

An important issue the user needs to be aware of is that there is very little security associated with MIDlet deployment. It is very simple for MIDlets to pretend to do one thing when advertised and then to actually do something else when run. The only safe approach is to download MIDlets from trusted sources.

Version 2.0 of the MIDP specification ensures that HTTPS, the secure HTTP protocol, is supported for the growing area of m-commerce.

Hopefully, this whistle-stop tour of MIDlets has given you an appreciation of the power and potential of this rapidly growing area of programming. Applications are being developed in areas such as gaming, m-learning, m-commerce and location-aware applications such as finding the user's nearest petrol station.

SAQ 2

(a) Which methods must be present in a MIDlet?

(b) In what way is the role of the constructor in a MIDlet subsumed elsewhere and what are the implications of this?

(c) Why might a MIDlet move into the paused state?

ANSWERS ....

(a) A MIDlet must have the `startApp`, `pauseApp` and `destroyApp` methods.

(b) One of the roles of the constructor is to carry out initializations. With MIDlets, this role is often carried out in the `startApp` method. As the `startApp` method will always be invoked, the developer has the choice of where to locate initialization code. One important implication of this is that because the `startApp` method may be called many times in the lifetime of a MIDlet, care must be taken to avoid unintended repeat initializations occurring.

(c) When created, a MIDlet initially moves into the paused state. After this, it can return to the paused state either by its invoking the `pauseApp` method or by the AMS forcing the MIDlet into pause, typically because of an incoming phone call.

SAQ 3

What are the three mechanisms through which a user can initiate action in J2ME and on which type of user interface can each one be used?

ANSWER...

The three types of user interaction are commands, item state changes and key handling. Commands and item state changes are available on high level user interfaces, and commands and key handling are available on low level user interfaces.

4 Servlets

We have seen that Java can be used to write independent applications and for applets that run on the client side of a web client–server system. Java can also be used very effectively on the web server side of a client–server system.

Early web systems had some limited interactivity, using the concept of web forms. Most web users will have seen these online forms, when filling in personal details to log on to some system or perhaps to buy something over the web. The HTML code to display a web form is run by the browser on the client. However, there is clearly a need to process the form information and perhaps store it – this is done on the server. This processing of HTML form data can be done in many different languages: C++, Perl and Java have all been used. In these early systems, this processing was done following a set of standard rules called **CGI** or the Common Gateway Interface. In many modern web-based systems CGI has been replaced by more efficient technology – for Java-based systems, we use Java **servlets**, which are part of the J2EE specification.

In this section, we shall see how servlets can be used for processing data from HTML forms, but also for many other purposes. We shall also see broadly how servlets are written. Because it is not within the scope of this course, we will not actually ask you to write any servlet code, but we will include some information that allows you to follow this up independently, if you wish to do so.

4.1 What is a servlet?

A servlet is a module of Java code that is stored and run on a web server. Many modern software systems are web-based applications – the user runs a browser to access a system over the web, and the bulk of the code that implements the application runs on a web server. Such applications can use Java servlets to implement a wide variety of functions, such as processing data, accessing databases and constructing complex web pages dynamically for return to the client.

Servlets are written in normal Java and so can make use of the full power of the Java language and its standard packages. Because they run on a server, whose security environment can be defined and controlled, they are not subject to the sort of security restrictions that limit the usefulness of standard applets. So, for example, servlets can access databases on the computer that hosts them or on a database server running on another computer. This is very useful in implementing the sort of 3-tier system we encountered in *Unit 9*.

Servlets also have the advantage of separating the user interface of a web application (which runs on the client) from the processing and database access. This can make it easier to change one or the other of these aspects of the system independently. Finally, by carrying out much of the processing on a sufficiently powerful server, the client software can be kept simple and responsive – a so-called **thin client**. Of course, if the server system is lacking in resources, this may introduce a bottleneck into the system, with clients waiting a relatively long time for service. The resource capacity of the various elements of a web-based system should be carefully designed to minimize this possibility. Figure 19 shows how a web application, using servlets, might be configured.

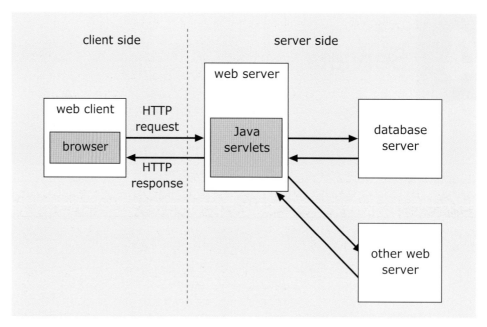

Figure 19   Web application with server running Java servlets

4.2 How do servlets work?

In *Unit 9*, we introduced the HTTP protocol for communication between web clients and web servers. We listed some of the important HTTP commands, such as GET and POST and gave some idea of the standard responses to these. We can now look 'behind the scenes' at what happens on the server side after the arrival of an HTTP request in order to construct the HTTP response.

We have discussed static web pages where the content does not change, unless the whole page is replaced. When a browser requests a static web page, using a GET command, the web server responds with HTTP header information (see *Unit 9* for details) followed by the HTML content of the web page, together with any associated files, such as multimedia files or applet code.

When we want to do something more complex like using the web server to process some data from an online form or to construct a web page dynamically in response to some specific request, the web server can use one or more servlets. The servlet runs on the web server in a software environment known as a **servlet container**. The Tomcat system, which was developed as part of the open source Apache Jakarta project, is freely available software that provides servlet containers and a web server.

See http://jakarta.apache.
org for details of the
Apache Jakarta project.

The servlet code accepts the HTTP request and any associated data, and constructs an appropriate HTTP response which is then sent back to the web client. If the request is successful, the response will mainly consist of a web page, possibly constructed dynamically by the servlet. In this way, servlets can return web pages that are adapted to the information supplied by the user, or containing information retrieved from other sources, such as a database.

Figure 19 shows an example of a web client sending an HTTP request to a web server. The web server is running one or more Java servlets and also interacts with a database server and a remote web server. Using the information from these sources, the servlets construct an HTTP response, consisting of header information, normally followed by a web page.

Coding of Java servlets has some similarities to the coding of applets although, of course, the environments for running servlets and applets respectively are quite different. A servlet is written as a class that extends the abstract `HttpServlet` class from the package `javax.servlet.http`. This package also defines the interfaces `HttpServletRequest` and `HttpServletResponse`. The `HttpServlet` class has a number of standard methods, which can be overridden to define the action of the servlet on receipt of various HTTP requests. Table 3 shows some of the important methods of this class.

Table 3 Important methods of the `HttpServlet` class

Method	Description
init	invoked by the servlet container to allocate and initialize resources when the servlet is first loaded
service	invoked by the servlet container when an HTTP request for service is received
doGet	a helper method, invoked by the `service` method when an HTTP GET request is received
doOptions	a helper method, invoked by the `service` method when an HTTP OPTIONS request is received – indicates the HTTP requests to which this server can respond
doPost	a helper method, invoked by the `service` method when an HTTP POST request is received
destroy	invoked to release resources and otherwise clean up, just before the servlet is removed from service

To write a servlet class, you must extend the `HttpServlet` class. Although this is an abstract class, it contains implementations for all its methods, but many of them do nothing or would simply cause the web server to return an error status to the web client. Hence, in most cases, you must override the methods you need, to ensure that the servlet responds to expected HTTP requests.

The `init` and `destroy` methods are invoked once each during the execution of the servlet, to initialize and clean up respectively – this is similar to the corresponding methods for applets. If you need initialization or clean-up you must override the relevant method. The `destroy` method would typically be used to close any open files or streams or to terminate any running threads.

Usually, the implementation of the `service` method is exactly what is needed and you need not override it. Its main function is to pass HTTP requests to one of a series of helper methods, each corresponding to one of the HTTP commands. So, for example, when a GET request is received, the service method passes this, together with any other data received, to the `doGet` method. Similarly, the `doPost` method handles any POST requests, and so on. The bad news is that the default implementation of most of the various `do` methods simply returns an error status as the response to be sent to the web client. You must override any of these methods required to ensure that the servlet can respond appropriately to any expected HTTP requests. An important exception to this is the `doOptions` method, which is fully implemented – it constructs the response to the HTTP OPTIONS request and causes the web server to indicate which HTTP requests it can respond to.

4.3 A simple example of servlet coding

To illustrate the previous discussion, we shall consider how to write a servlet that will respond to a simple request for dynamically generated data. The example we shall consider is a request for a set of randomly generated numbers, such as might be required for a lottery. In a lottery, participants normally have to select a set of numbers with each number being within a given range. They also have to pay a small amount to enter the lottery. A central system then randomly generates a set of winning numbers, and the one or more people who chose exactly those numbers win or share the lottery prize, which is often a large sum of money.

In this first example, the client system will ask the server to respond with a suitable set of numbers to be entered in the lottery. At this stage, we assume that the rest of the lottery process is handled elsewhere – this system simply helps the lottery player to identify a set of suitable 'lucky' numbers. Later we will add more features, making the system a little more realistic.

This lottery requires players to choose a set of four integers, each between 1 and 99 inclusive. Hence, all the servlet needs to do is to generate four suitable random integers and to return these on a web page to the client. Admittedly, we could just as easily generate these numbers using an applet, or in JavaScript, but consider this simple servlet as a base for further functions to be added later. For simplicity, we ignore the (real) possibility of duplicate random numbers being generated.

As we have seen, a servlet is written as a class that extends the abstract `HttpServlet` class. In this case we expect the client to issue an HTTP `GET` request, so we must override the `doGet` method to provide a suitable web page in response.

The code for the `LotteryLuckyNumbersServlet` is as follows.

```
public class LotteryLuckyNumbersServlet extends HttpServlet
{
    final static int NUMBER_OF_VALUES = 4;
    final static int MAX_VALUE = 99; // numbers from 1 to this

    Random random; // random number generator
    int [] value; // lucky number values

    /* Initialize the random number generator
    and set up an array for the lucky numbers.*/
    public void init ()
    {
        random = new Random();
        value = new int [NUMBER_OF_VALUES];
    }

    public void doGet (HttpServletRequest req, HttpServletResponse resp)
        throws ServletException, IOException
    {
        // generate the random lucky numbers
        for (int i = 0; i < NUMBER_OF_VALUES; i++)
        {
            value [i] = random.nextInt(MAX_VALUE) + 1;
        }
```

```
// send them back in a web page
resp.setContentType("text/HTML");
PrintWriter out = resp.getWriter();
out.println("<HTML>");
out.println("<HEAD>");
out.println("<TITLE>Lucky Numbers</TITLE>");
out.println("</HEAD>");
out.println("<BODY>");
out.println("<H1>Walrus Lottery</H1>");
out.println("<BR> <BR>");
out.println("<H2>Your lucky numbers are:</H2>");
out.println("<BR> <BR> <H1>");

for (int i = 0; i < NUMBER_OF_VALUES; i++)
{
    out.print (value [i] + " ");
}

out.println("</H1>");
out.println("<BR> <BR>");
out.println("<H2>Wishing you the best of luck</H2>");
out.println("<BR> <HR> <BR>");
out.println("<H4>We do not guarantee a winning result</H4>");
out.println("<H4>Walruses can go down as well as up</H4>");
out.println("</BODY>");
out.println("</HTML>");
out.flush();
out.close();
    }
}
```

The class defines two public methods, `init` and `doGet`, each of which overrides a default implementation. The `init` method runs once when the servlet is first activated. In this case, it creates and initializes the random number generator object as well as setting up an array to hold the lucky numbers.

The `doGet` method constructs and sends the response to a GET request from the client. This method has two arguments, `req` and `resp`, that reference objects corresponding to the request data received and the response to be constructed, respectively. In this simple case, there is no additional data associated with the request so the `req` argument is not used. The response object is used to send the reply.

In this case, there is no need to override the `destroy` method as there are no resources to release apart from the objects created by the `init` method – these will be dealt with by Java garbage collection in the normal way.

The servlet sends back an HTTP response consisting of a header, indicating the type of content (text and HTML), followed by the source of the web page as follows:

```
<HTML>
    <HEAD>
        <TITLE>Lucky Numbers</TITLE>
    </HEAD>
    <BODY>
        <H1>Walrus Lottery</H1>
        <BR> <BR>
        <H2>Your lucky numbers are:</H2>
        <BR> <BR>
        <H1>4 21 52 47</H1>
        <BR> <BR>
        <H2>Wishing you the best of luck</H2>
        <BR> <HR> <BR>
        <H4>We do not guarantee a winning result</H4>
        <H4>Walruses can go down as well as up</H4>
    </BODY>
</HTML>
```

Of course, the lucky numbers that are returned will vary with each response. This is why a static web page cannot be used in this case. When viewed using a browser, this web page is as shown in Figure 20.

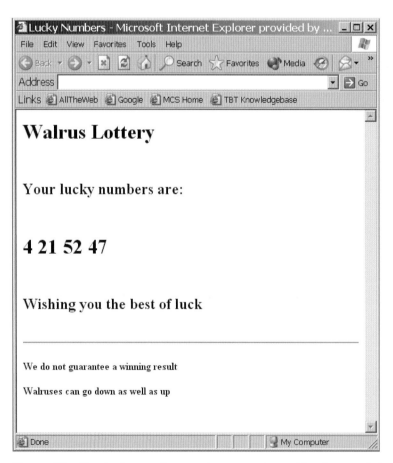

Figure 20   The lucky numbers web page returned by the servlet

4.4 Using a servlet to respond to user input

We extend the previous example to show how to write a servlet that will process data from an HTML form. As we noted earlier, servlets are versatile and can also be applied to many other activities.

First, we must briefly explain HTML forms. Most people will have used online forms as they are commonly used for input of personal data when making purchases or subscribing to organizations or events on the web. An area of a web page can be defined as a form, by a section of HTML enclosed in <FORM> and </FORM> tags. A web page can have one or more forms, defined within the body of the HMTL page. Between the <FORM> and </FORM> tags, normal text or other HTML tags can be used. In addition, there are special tags that can define user interface components such as text fields, command buttons, option buttons, and so on.

Let us create a simple form that allows a user to log in to the lottery system introduced above. This will prove useful later when we consider how the system could be used to actually submit a lottery entry. In a real online lottery system a form might have lots of security features, help systems and sophisticated layout but, for this example, we shall keep the information and the form layout very simple.

Figure 21 shows how the form would look, when viewed using a browser.

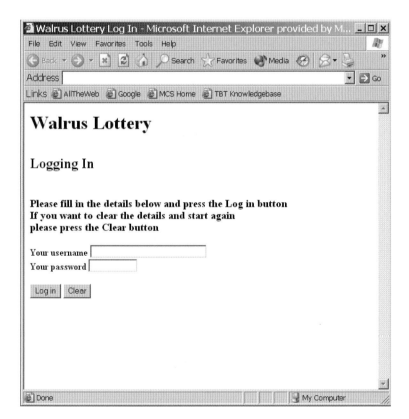

Figure 21   The HTML form page for logging in, viewed using a browser

The HTML required for the form part of this web page is as follows.

```
<FORM METHOD = "POST" ACTION = "/servlet/WalrusLottery/LotteryLogin">
    Your username
    <INPUT TYPE = "TEXT" NAME = "USERNAME" SIZE = "30"> <BR>
    Your password
    <INPUT TYPE = "PASSWORD" NAME = "PASSWORD" SIZE = "10"> <BR>
    <BR>
    <INPUT TYPE = "SUBMIT" NAME = "LOGIN" VALUE = "Log In">
    <INPUT TYPE = "RESET" NAME = "RESETLOGIN" VALUE = "Clear">
</FORM>
```

In order to concentrate on the structure of the form, we have omitted the standard HTML to set up the head and body parts of the web page and to display the supporting text at the start of the page. The <FORM> tag contains two attributes. The METHOD attribute indicates that the result of sending the form will be an HTTP POST request. The ACTION attribute specifies that this request will be processed by a servlet called LotteryLogin in the WalrusLottery domain.

The two text fields are defined using the <INPUT> tags with appropriate type parameters. For the user name field, the TYPE parameter is set to "TEXT" while for the password field, the type parameter is set to "PASSWORD" to ensure that the contents are not displayed when the user fills in this field. The SIZE parameter specifies the size of the text field in number of characters, although normally the text field will scroll to allow additional characters beyond this limit. The NAME parameter specifies a name for the text field – this will be used by the servlet that processes the data. Each <INPUT> tag is preceded by some plain text to tell the user what to input.

Two of the standard button types associated with forms are specified by setting the TYPE attribute of the <INPUT> tag to "SUBMIT" or "RESET" respectively, as shown above. When the SUBMIT button is clicked, the HTTP request specified in the <FORM> tag (in this case, a POST request) is sent for processing. The RESET button clears all the text fields on the form, allowing the user to start filling in data again, normally because the data was completely wrong. The user sees these buttons labelled as the Login button and the Clear button respectively, as defined by the VALUE attribute of the <INPUT> tag.

The response we expect after submitting this form will be a web page, with two possible outcomes. If there was missing or erroneous information, we could expect a page with an error message, indicating what had gone wrong. If all was well, we would expect a web page confirming a valid login and inviting the user to proceed with their lottery entry. To keep this example simple, we shall assume that a successful login results in the servlet sending back a set of lucky numbers, as before.

The servlet class LotteryLogin needs the following structure.

▶ Inherits from class HttpServlet.

▶ Overrides the doPost method.

▶ Checks that all input data is present and corresponds to the previously registered user name and password.

▶ Returns a suitable error page if any data is missing or erroneous.

▶ If the data is correct, it returns a web page confirming the login and containing a set of 'lucky numbers'.

The start of the code for the class `LotteryLogin` is as follows.

```
public class LotteryLogin extends HttpServlet
{
public void doPost(HttpServletRequest req, HttpServletResponse resp)
    throws ServletException, IOException
{
    try
    {
        UserData user = getUserData(req);
        sendLuckyNumbers(resp, user);
    }
    catch (BadUserDataException e)
    {
        sendErrorReport(resp, e);
    }
}
...
```

This shows the only public method of the servlet, `doPost`, which constructs and sends the response to a `POST` request from the client. This method has two parameters that reference objects corresponding to the request data received and the response to be constructed respectively. The code above uses three helper methods, `getUserData`, `sendLuckyNumbers` and `sendErrorReport` to do all the work. We shall look at these in more detail below but, briefly, the operation of the `doPost` method is as follows. It invokes the `getUserData` method to check the data input onto the form by the user and to store this in a `UserData` object. If there are any problems with the data, the method will throw a `BadUserDataException`, which is handled by the `catch` clause of the `doPost` method. If the data is valid, the `doPost` method will invoke the method `sendLuckyNumbers` to send back a set of numbers, as before. If an exception occurs due to bad input data then the method `sendErrorReport` will be invoked to send a suitable response page. Clearly, this is a rather simplistic approach, but we are mainly concerned with demonstrating the basic principle of servlets here.

An outline of the helper method `getUserData` is as follows.

```
private UserData getUserData (HttpServletRequest req)
    throws BadUserDataException
{
    UserData user = new UserData();
    String userName = req.getParameter("USERNAME");

    if (userName.length() == 0)
    {
        throw BadUserDataException("Invalid user name");
    }
    user.setName(username);
    String userPassword = req.getParameter("PASSWORD");

    if (userPassword.length() == 0)
    {
        throw BadUserDataException("Invalid password");
    }
    user.setPassword(userPassword);
    return user;
}
```

Again, this method takes a very simplistic approach. In a more realistic example, it would check the user name and password against values previously stored in a database. The obvious errors of blank user name or password could also be more efficiently detected using JavaScript code running on the client system. However, this method does show the basic approach to extracting data from the HTTP request object, using the `getParameter` method. This method returns a `String` corresponding to the specified item on the HTML form. Consider the following line from the method code above:

```
String userName = req.getParameter("USERNAME");
```

This extracts the value entered in the text field labelled `"USERNAME"` by the following line that we saw earlier in the HTML form:

```
<INPUT TYPE = "TEXT" NAME = "USERNAME" SIZE = "30"> <BR>
```

If the `getUserData` method finds any errors in the input data, it throws an exception including a suitable error message that can ultimately be returned to the user. We omit details of the class `UserData`, but its general structure should be clear from the above code examples.

Returning to the `doPost` method again, remember that it invokes one of two other helper methods to send a response back to the client. We briefly indicate here how these might work, without going into detailed code.

The `sendLuckyNumbers` method would be almost identical to the code in the `doGet` method of the class `LotteryLuckyNumbersServlet` in Subsection 4.3 above. In this case, it would also be possible to confirm the successful log in and to display the user name as part of the response. An alternative approach would be for this method to pass the request on to the `LotteryLuckyNumbersServlet`, which could be running on the same server or even on a different server – the details of this are beyond the scope of this unit.

The `sendErrorReport` method could simply return a standard static web page indicating a log in error. It would be more helpful to the user if this method were to construct a dynamic web page, containing the error message associated with the `BadUserDataException`. In the next subsection, we shall see that a servlet may not be the best way to achieve this, and that the related technology of Java Server Pages (JSP) is more appropriate in this case.

4.5 Servlets and JSP

It should be clear from the previous sections that servlets are very powerful – they have access to the full Java language for any processing required at the server in response to HTTP requests. However, much of the response to most requests is likely to consist of static elements defining the text, graphics and layout of the response web page. Writing these static elements to the output stream using a servlet is a rather awkward way to proceed. This can also make it harder to maintain such web pages and requires the attention of Java programmers rather than web page designers.

To address these problems, there is a very useful technology called **Java Server Pages** (usually known as **JSP**). A JSP is like a static page of HTML and text, but may also contain sections of Java code, indicated by special tags. If there is a lot of static HTML code in the response, it is worth using a JSP to construct the response page. The following code is the JSP required for the lucky numbers response page created using a servlet in Subsection 4.3:

```
<HTML>
    <HEAD>
        <TITLE>Lucky Numbers</TITLE>
    </HEAD>
    <BODY>
        <H1>Walrus Lottery</H1>
        <BR> <BR>
        <H2>Your lucky numbers are:</H2>
        <BR> <BR>
        <H1>
        <%@ page import = "java.util.*" %>
        <% Random random = new Random();
            for (int i = 0; i < 4; i++)
            {
                out.println(random.nextInt(MAX_VALUE) + 1);
            }
        %>
        </H1>
        <BR> <BR>
        <H2>Wishing you the best of luck</H2>
        <BR> <HR> <BR>
        <H4>We do not guarantee a winning result</H4>
        <H4>Walruses can go down as well as up</H4>
    </BODY>
</HTML>
```

This is almost identical to the source of the page sent back by the servlet in Subsection 4.3, except that the JSP contains the Java code needed to produce the dynamically generated part. The Java code section, known as a **scriptlet**, is enclosed in the special tags `<%` and `%>`. Note the slightly different, but recognizable, form of the `import` statement, which also uses special tags `<%@` and `%>`.

In fact, when the JSP is processed, this simply creates an appropriate servlet to build the required response page. The JSP is stored in a normal text file, with a name ending in `.jsp`. A JSP can be directly accessed from a browser by entering its URL or clicking on a link, or it can be invoked by a servlet in constructing its response to a request. In the example above in Subsection 4.4, the method `sendErrorReport` could usefully be implemented to invoke a JSP with standard error reporting content together with dynamically generated information about the details of the error. The details of how servlets and JSPs communicate are outside the scope of this unit, but the principles should be clear.

To summarize:

▶   if an HTTP response requires mostly HTML and a little bit of processing, use a JSP;

▶   if an HTTP response requires mostly processing and a little static HTML, use a servlet;

▶   often a good approach is to use both servlets and JSP, applying the strengths of each approach, and separating the processing from the user interface details.

4.6 Servlets and databases

Applets can, as we have seen, 'phone home' to access stored data on the server from which they were downloaded, but cannot normally access the file system on the client system where they execute. One of the advantages of servlets over standard applets is that servlets can access stored data on the local server or on any linked computer. This is often most conveniently handled by having a servlet access information stored in a database, as shown in Figure 22.

For example, in the lottery example above, the log in process really should access stored details of the user name and password to ensure a valid log in. It would also be useful to allow a lottery player to enter their chosen lottery numbers and store these in a database, to be checked later against the winning numbers. Figure 22 shows how Java programs, including servlets, can access a range of standard database systems using the technology known as **JDBC**.

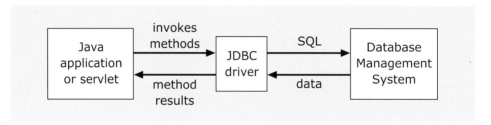

Figure 22   How Java applications or servlets access a database

You might have thought that JDBC stands for something like Java Database Connectivity, but it officially stands for JDBC™, according to Sun Microsystems. JDBC is a set of classes, structured into packages, that provides an API for accessing databases from Java programs. It has the advantage that it works with a variety of databases, and it is even possible to change the database used by a JDBC-based Java program without changing the Java source code. A software component known as a **JDBC driver** provides the interface between the Java program and the **database management system** (**DBMS**). The JDBC driver for a specific DBMS, such as Oracle or Access, communicates with the DBMS in the specific language required by that DBMS. The DBMS may be on the same computer or running on a separate server from the Java program and on a completely different platform – it makes no difference, except perhaps to the speed of response if the database server is on a distant or slow communications link.

The details of JDBC are outside the scope of this course. However, we can follow the broad outline of how it works. Servlets construct database queries by invoking Java methods from the JDBC API. These generate **SQL queries** and send the queries to a database management system. **SQL** (Standard Query Language) is used to request or modify data stored by database management systems, and is standard in that it is implemented by all major database products. SQL is not so standard because particular database manufacturers tend to add their own variants and extensions to the standard language. Each DBMS may also differ in the types of data it can conveniently handle, such as integers, decimal numbers, dates, times or money. Hence, there is a need for a JDBC driver specific to each particular DBMS. JDBC also deals with receiving the data returned by the DBMS and packaging it for retrieval by the Java program that requested it. The data is normally returned as a result object from a method invocation.

When writing servlets to access a database, it is normally useful to override the `init` method to set up access to the database, and to release the link to the database using the `destroy` method, just before the servlet terminates.

Incidentally, communication that is intended to be secure against corruption or interception normally uses a more secure protocol than standard HTTP, such as the **HTTPS** protocol (HTTP Secure). This would be essential, for example, where financial information such as a credit card number is to be transmitted.

SAQ 4

How can servlets and JSPs be used to respond to user inputs to a web page?

ANSWER...

Servlets are pure Java programs that run in a servlet container on a web server. Simple JSPs are a mixture of HTML and sections of Java code. Before a JSP is executed, it is first compiled to a Java servlet.

A servlet that responds to HTTP requests is defined as a class that extends the class `HttpServlet` and makes use of objects of the classes `HttpRequest` and `HttpResponse`. To deal with any expected HTTP commands, such as `GET` and `POST`, it must define corresponding methods (in this case, `doGet` and `doPost` respectively). These methods override inherited versions of `doGet`, `doPost`, and so on. They contain the code that extracts any user data sent with the HTTP request and constructs an appropriate HTTP response object, typically in the form of a dynamically constructed web page. This web page may contain data extracted from a database, accessed using JDBC.

Servlets and JSPs can invoke other servlets and JSPs to carry out part of the required processing. JSPs are useful for responses that require mainly static HTML with a limited amount of variable content, defined by their Java sections.

5 Aglets

This section looks at an application of Java technology that is in some way still in a developmental stage and has not yet been taken up commercially to any great extent. However, it offers some interesting possibilities. This is the technology of aglets.

5.1 What is an aglet?

The word aglet follows the tradition begun by applet (a small application, app–let) and is a contraction of agent (ag – let). It is also the word for the little metal tags on the ends of shoe laces.

An **aglet** is an autonomous mobile agent, which is able to move from one computer to another computer carrying along with itself state information and executable code. On arrival at another computer it is able to run itself and carry out whatever task it was designed to do and then, if necessary, move to another computer spawning copies of itself if needed.

The term agent is used in many ways but the general sense intended here is a piece of software that 'helps somebody do something', such as find the best price for an item on the internet. The key feature about aglets though is that both the state and the code are mobile. They are autonomous in the sense that once released with a task to carry out they are able to decide where they will go. They are able to interact with the server that they are currently running on and with other aglets. They can halt their execution on one server, travel across a network and then resume execution on another server with their state information and code intact.

Aglets have been described as a development of the object-oriented programming paradigm in that as well as an object having state, behaviour and identity, it also has location. With aglets, executable content is moved across a network and can be regarded as a distributed object that is able to move.

IBM's work on aglets can be accessed from http://www.trl.ibm.com

While still largely developmental there are a number of toolkits for the creation of aglets, one of the most popular being IBM's Aglets Workbench. This contains its own agent APIs for creating Java-based mobile agent applications. We do not have the space here to be able to go into the code level details but there are many resources available on the internet for further information.

5.2 Mobility

At first glance, an aglet might seem to be similar to an applet. The class files for an applet can travel across a network and then run. However, the aglet differs in two important ways – the aglet carries information about its state and it is not limited to travelling from a server to a client to run, it can and usually does move from server to server. As it has state information, it can follow a particular itinerary and return to its original host.

In order to be able to do this, the aglet requires a particular type of server – an aglet host. The migration from one server to another is only possible if the servers are aglet hosts. Each host has a security manager to ensure that the activities of the visiting aglet do not act in a way detrimental to the host. This is one of the reasons that Java has been so strongly identified with aglets. As well as providing platform independence, it also provides 'sandbox' security against possible malicious code.

5.3 Host servers and the server context

As we have seen above, aglets are able to move executable code onto a compatible server. The general approach is that a suitably configured server will create a **server context** within which aglets are able to insert themselves and run. The context itself is stationary and provides an environment for hosting and managing visiting aglets and providing protection for the host server from malicious code. In a sense, the context can be thought of as an enclave within a host country. Travellers are able to visit the enclave and go about their business there, but they are not able to interact with the wider population directly. Instead, the enclave provides the services that the traveller needs through secure intermediaries with the wider population. In the same way, through the services provided by the context, an aglet is able to get information about the environment and send and receive messages; it is also able to interact with other aglets in the context.

When arriving at a host server, the aglet will present its identity for verification and then obtain from the context, access to local services and data. Aglets within the same context are also able to interact and invoke each other's methods. There is the potential for this to happen synchronously or asynchronously, thus allowing for a very flexible form of information exchange. Again, using the traveller analogy, if a traveller posts a message on a noticeboard within the enclave, then a fellow traveller standing at the noticeboard at the same time can read it as it is being posted. However, the notice can also be read several months later by any passing traveller with an interest in that topic.

After spending some time in a context, the aglet can then decide to move on based either on current developments or a pre-planned itinerary.

This is a different form of distributed application than you might have met before. The traditional paradigm is for static code to use an object at another location (a remote object) to achieve a result. With aglets, the code itself moves to the other location. In a sense, it is the difference between asking someone in another place to do something for you (remote object) and going there and doing it for yourself (aglets).

5.4 | Aglet life events

Different models of aglets suggest slightly different events that can occur in the life cycle of an aglet. Table 4 gives a broad view of what might happen.

Table 4   Aglet life events

Event	Description
Create	construction of a new aglet with all of the attendant initialization and preparation for execution
Dispatch	the aglet moves from one host to another, which can be initiated either by the aglet itself or, for example, by another aglet asking it to move
Arrive	the aglet arrives at a new host and, after verification procedures, begins to execute in the new context
Dispose	preparation for termination, including the release of any resources held
Clone	an aglet is duplicated, usually in order to move to several hosts at once

5.5 | Aglet applications

As well as representing a more abstract view of programming as suggested above, there are many application for which aglets have been proposed as being particularly suited. These applications make use of the fact that aglets take their executable code with them and hold state information.

An aglet might be used, for example, to negotiate buying a car for you. As aglet technology spreads there could well be aglet host servers that specialize in the buying and selling of particular products. If there was one that specialized in selling cars, you could give your aglet information about your preferences including, for example, a price range, model and colour and even a strategy for haggling. You would send your aglet to the host server, where it would interact with other aglets that were trying to sell a car. Your aglet could report back to you if a possible deal was found or could do the deal for you especially if an instant decision was needed to get a bargain.

To end this section, we list below some of the other possible applications of aglets to whet your appetite:

▶   data collection from distributed sites;

▶   monitoring events at remote sites;

▶   'spam' aglets – sending targeted information to host sites;

▶   'guard' aglets to filter out Spam aglets;

▶   scheduling aglets – arranging meetings;

▶   cloning to produce parallel processing.

SAQ 5

(a) What four properties do aglet objects have?

(b) When it comes to creating and using aglets, what two advantages does Java offer over other languages?

ANSWERS ....

(a) Aglets have state, behaviour, identity and location.

(b) Java offers portability and 'sandbox' security.

---

6 Hardware Java

Many modern technological devices or systems contain computer systems to enable them to work although the device or system, as a whole, has a wider purpose and would not be regarded as a computer system. From the computing point of view, such devices or systems are known as embedded devices or **embedded systems** – they contain a computer system embedded within them.

Java is now used or planned to be used in many embedded devices, such as medical equipment, printers, TV set-top boxes or car engine management. This is an interesting return to the roots of Java – it was originally devised as a language to be used for networked embedded devices. It was not immediately successful in this role and, for some time, Java became a solution in search of a problem. Like many inventions, it initially found application in a completely different area from that envisaged by its developers. It became extremely popular first for use in applets on the web and then as a general purpose programming language.

In this section, we briefly survey how Java is being used or adapted for embedded systems.

6.1 Embedded systems

Embedded systems are different from normal J2SE applications or even J2ME games and applications on phones and PDAs because, in these latter cases, we usually know we are running a program on a sort of computer. An embedded system does not normally look like a computer, but looks like a printer or a camera or whatever the containing device may be.

Embedded systems often have rather specialized and possibly demanding requirements. They may be small in physical size, with limited resources of memory or processing power, as we have seen for J2ME systems. They are often used to monitor and control equipment and so may need to operate as **real-time systems**.

A real-time system is a computer system that needs to respond within specified time limits in order to function properly. Some real-time systems, known as hard real-time systems, cannot permit any time deadline to be missed – failure to meet a deadline may be regarded as a failure of the system, possibly with serious consequences for the equipment being controlled or for human life. For example, modern road vehicles are often fitted with air bags that should inflate in the case of an accident, or automatic braking systems (ABS) which help drivers to stop quickly and safely. Both these systems are controlled by embedded computers and the timing of their responses is critical – there is no point in the air bag inflating correctly several seconds after a crash. Other systems may have timing requirements, but occasional missed deadlines may be acceptable – these are known as soft real-time systems. Many multimedia systems are of this type – for example, occasional late or missed frames in a video stream are normally acceptable.

We saw in a previous section that small scale systems, with limited resources, are to some extent catered for by J2ME. This does not, however, address the special needs of real-time systems. These include:

▶ predictable timing behaviour of code;

▶ threads are useful but must be managed carefully to avoid blocking and deadlock, and to allow prediction of their timing behaviour;

▶ Java garbage collection can disrupt time-critical activities;

▶ systems may be safety-critical or need very high reliability;

▶ some systems may require high performance from limited resources – standard Java's use of interpreted bytecode may be a problem here.

Because of this, there has been a considerable amount of work over several years on developing specifications for a **real-time Java**. This has been associated with a fair amount of politics, such as rival working groups from different sets of manufacturers, but these differences have now been settled. The outcome was a standard specification of what is required from a real-time version of Java – the Real-time Specification for Java or **RTSJ**. There are also a number of products that comply with some or all of the requirements of RTSJ. The products typically involve a special class library, a specialized compiler and other development tools, and special versions of the Java Virtual Machine (JVM) that run the Java programs on the embedded devices.

RTSJ

The Real-time Specification for Java defines a special class library, `javax.realtime`, containing a variety of classes that address many of the limitations of standard Java in relation to real-time programming. Some examples of these specializations are as follows.

The RTSJ `RealtimeThread` class extends `java.lang.Thread`. This provides a larger range of thread priorities (at least 28 levels) and supports a variety of scheduling approaches appropriate for real-time systems. This makes the timing behaviour of threads more predictable.

The potential problems of Java garbage collection for time-critical code are addressed by defining several different kinds of memory to be used for data storage. *Immortal memory* is used for data that is needed throughout the program; *scoped memory* (such as local variables in a method) is automatically freed at the end of a defined scope (such as the end of the method execution). Threads can be defined to use only immortal or scoped memory. In this way, garbage collection can largely be avoided.

A `RawMemory` class allows reading and writing of integer or floating-point data at specific memory addresses – this is sometimes used in embedded systems to access particular hardware devices. RTSJ also specifies a set of classes for dealing with time and timers, potentially using very short time periods such as 1 nanosecond, if the implementation supports this.

Clearly, RTSJ introduces some additional complexity into standard Java. However, this is a necessary price to pay in order to apply the advantages of the Java language in the more demanding environment of real-time systems. Even RTSJ is not entirely adequate for safety-critical systems – at present this is an area of active research and development.

More information about the RTSJ can be found at http://www.rtj.org.

We have seen that execution of Java code is normally a two-stage process of compilation followed by interpretation, as shown in Figure 23.

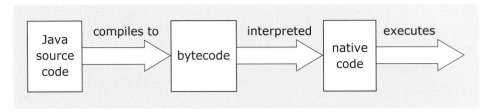

Figure 23   The standard Java compilation and interpretation process

This two-stage execution process may result in relatively slow execution, which is unacceptable in some real-time systems. Compilers may overcome these performance limitations in one of two ways. **Native compilers** translate Java source code directly into the native code required by the processor on the embedded device, thus cutting out the bytecode interpretation process, as shown in Figure 24. This may improve performance and reduce the memory required to run Java program, when compared to the normal process of interpretation by the JVM. However, it does lose the major advantage of Java bytecode being platform independent.

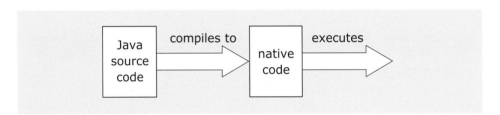

Figure 24   The action of a Java native code compiler

Just-in-time (JIT) compilers operate by compiling parts of the Java program through to native code, but each part is compiled only just before it is first required for execution. This can be particularly effective if that part of the program is executed repeatedly, for example, in a loop. Figure 25 illustrates this process. These sort of tools mean that Java can achieve high performance if required in embedded systems.

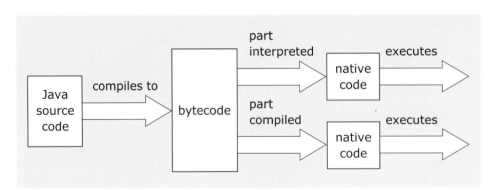

Figure 25   The action of a Java JIT compiler

6.2 Embedded systems example

For quite some time, television (TV) set-top boxes have been used for cable TV and, more recently, have been used in connection with digital TV from cable, satellite or broadcast sources. A set-top box contains a processor and memory and is connected between the TV and the source of TV signals as well as to some sort of return connection for data. This connection may be a telephone line via cable, normal copper wires, or possibly satellite, as shown in Figure 26.

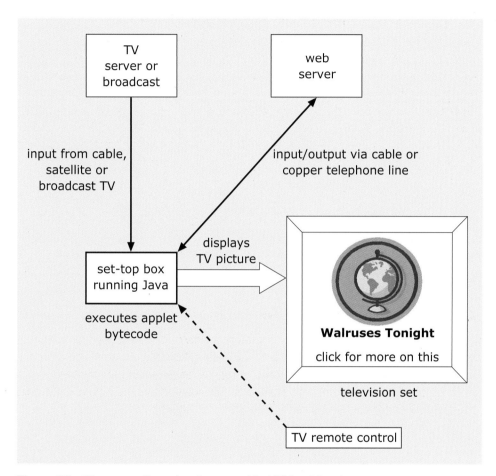

Figure 26   The operation of a Java-enabled TV set-top box

Modern set-top boxes may have quite considerable processor and memory resources and run software to allow functions such as tuning, TV programme information, access to pay TV, video on demand, interactive TV, and ecommerce.

Set-top boxes use a wide variety of different processors, often specially designed for embedded systems. Java's cross-platform capabilities make it useful for addressing this diverse range of hardware. It is also useful to be able to download software updates or additional functions easily across the cable network or other communications links. Java-enabled set-top boxes can run Java applets effectively because the fast cable or other broadband connection minimizes any delay in downloading the applet code. Another advantage is that Java applications such as browsers or ecommerce systems, written for completely different platforms, such as PCs or PDAs may be readily adapted to run on set-top boxes.

There are Java standards for digital TV set-top boxes as part of J2ME CLDC. The OpenCable Applications Platform (OCAP) standard is aimed at newer digital set-top boxes with substantial resources – typically 8Mb of memory. There is also an emerging standard for the many older digital set-top boxes already in service that typically have fewer resources – perhaps 700Kb of memory or less.

Has Java been to Mars?

There have been a number of reports in recent times, suggesting that Java technology has been to Mars as part of a NASA space expedition. A closer reading indicates that these reports were, strictly speaking, a little premature.

NASA has landed a number of remotely controlled vehicles, known as rovers, on Mars in recent years. In 1997 the Sojourner rover was able to travel short distances, carrying out scientific measurements and returning detailed images to Earth. Early in 2004 two more rovers, Spirit and Opportunity, were landed at different locations on Mars and they travelled considerable distances, sending back a wealth of images and data. Java was used in the systems on Earth for planning and directing the progress of these two rovers. A similar system, called Maestro, (with simulations only, but using real data from Mars) was also freely available on the web for anyone wanting to understand more about the mission.

The systems on Mars directly controlling the rovers did not use Java.

However NASA's Jet Propulsion Laboratory (JPL) in California has, for some time, been developing an experimental new version of the Mars rover vehicle, called Rocky 7 (see below). The software for Rocky 7 does use real-time Java (RTSJ-compliant) to control its steering, navigation and other exploration components. So far, Rocky 7 has been tested in various desert environments on Earth but has not been to Mars.

Photograph copyright ©
Glenn Research Center,
NASA.

Activity 10.7
Find out how many devices worldwide are currently estimated to use Java technology and how this breaks down into different sorts of devices.

6.3 Java Card

Smart cards are small plastic cards containing electronic memory and some form of microprocessor. They may be credit-card sized, such as the cards commonly used to withdraw money from bank cash machines or to gain access to restricted areas of buildings. Smaller smart cards are used within mobile phones as SIM (Subscriber Identity Module) cards, to securely identify the user of the phone. Smart cards have also been used as identity cards, to store electronic cash for use in vending machines and other payment systems and as a replacement for tickets in public transport systems.

Smart cards can be contact cards or contactless cards. Contact cards must be physically inserted into a reader – the metal contacts on the card surface allow communication between the card and any systems linked to the card reader (see Figure 27). Contactless cards communicate using a short range radio signal and need only be brought near a reading device, without physical contact. Normally, smart cards do not contain a power source, but are powered up when connected to a card reader.

Figure 27   Example of a contact smart card (contacts on the right of the card)

Java Card is a technology defined by Sun Microsystems, which enables smart cards and similar devices with very limited resources to run small Java applications known as applets (but different from the standard Java applets we have seen previously). It uses a very restricted subset of the Java APIs, even more restricted than those defined for J2ME. Some of the advantages proposed by Sun for the Java Card technology are as follows.

▶ Java Card applets written for one type of smart card will run on any other card that uses the Java Card technology.

▶ The Java language and execution environment offer a high level of security.

▶ Several applets can coexist on the same card and new applications can be securely added to a previously issued card.

▶ Java Card technology complies with formal standards for smart cards.

A simple Java Card device has an 8-bit or 16-bit processor with a small amount (say, 1Kb) of RAM (volatile memory) and usually a larger amount (say, 16Kb) of non-volatile memory, such as EEPROM, which does not lose its contents when the card is powered off. More powerful cards may have a 32-bit processor, and a separate cryptographic chip and memory to perform the encryption operations that are essential for security applications.

The software that runs on the card consists of:

▶ the card operating system;

▶ a special JVM – the Java Card Virtual Machine that runs the applets;

▶ the Java Card API – Java classes that support smart card applications;

▶ the applet or applets for a specific application.

The software on the card is, of course, only part of the software required for a typical application. The Java Card device need only run enough software to fulfil its role of identifying the card holder, recording access rights or whatever the application requires.

More extensive processing can be done on other systems linked to the card via the card reader, as shown in Figure 28.

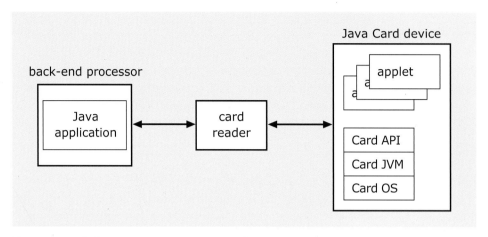

Figure 28   Software running on a Java Card device

Figure 28 shows a minimal configuration – there may be a host system local to the card reader and one or more back-end processors, perhaps at a remote site and running application servers, database servers, and so on. A typical system may also have many card reading devices at different locations. It should be possible for developers to use Java development tools to produce code right across this wide range of devices from servers to smart cards.

At the time of writing, hundreds of millions of smart cards based on Java Card technology had been deployed.

SAQ 6

What are the limitations of Java for real-time or embedded systems and how can these be overcome or accommodated?

ANSWER...

There are problems in respect of the following:

►   predictable timing behaviour of code;

►   threads are useful but must be managed carefully to avoid blocking and deadlock and to allow prediction of their timing behaviour;

►   Java garbage collection can disrupt time-critical activities;

►   systems may be safety-critical or need very high reliability;

►   some systems may require high performance from limited resources – standard Java's use of interpreted bytecode may be a problem here.

To address these problems, we can use a real-time Java environment, which has a special real-time JVM, such as that defined by RTSJ. Using a native or JIT compiler helps address possible performance problems in resource-constrained embedded systems.

7 Review

We have come to the end of the part of the course that teaches Java and have met the main concepts of the Java language and how it can be used in many different components. We have seen that the Java language can be used across a very wide range of platforms. Figure 29 gives an overview of the Java Technology concept map.

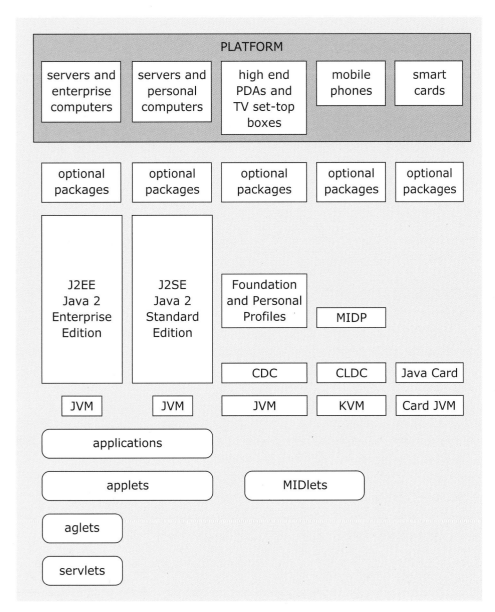

Figure 29   The Java Technology concept map

How does Java compare against the list of the language designers' aims that we saw in *Unit 1*? Before we attempt to answer this question, you may wish to answer it yourself. By now, you should at least understand what the aims mean!

Further details of the Java Technology concept map can be found at http://www.java.sun.com

SAQ 7

We summarize below the aims of the Java language designers, taken from their 'white paper' and discussed in *Unit 1*. The language was to be:

▶ simple;

▶ familiar;

▶ object-oriented;

▶ robust;

▶ secure;

▶ portable;

▶ high performance;

▶ interpreted;

▶ threaded;

▶ dynamic.

How well do you think Java has fulfilled these aims?

ANSWER..

Many of the points in this answer have been discussed in the course. In this SAQ answer, we have taken the liberty of adding some extra information and views that may go a little further than the material in the previous course units. Our comments on each aspect are as follows.

▶ Simple: Java has a small, consistent core of fundamental concepts although much of the power lies in the extensive class libraries, which take longer to learn.

▶ Familiar: Much of the language syntax resembles C and C++ ; perhaps it is less familiar to those with other experience. This resemblance has probably helped Java's rapid acceptance by experienced programmers, although there are subtle and possibly deceptive differences between Java and C++.

▶ Object-oriented: Java is definitely object-oriented – all programs are structured around objects, although not everything is an object. The use of primitive types like `int` and `char` means that Java is not a pure object-oriented language like Smalltalk, for example.

▶ Robust: Java programs are strictly checked by the compiler and exceptions, if properly handled, can aid robustness. Garbage collection and the absence of memory pointers eliminate a source of very common errors in other languages that require explicit management of memory for data.

▶ Secure: We have seen that Java applets have special security features to ensure that programs running over networks cannot damage your computer files or introduce viruses. Digital signatures can be applied to classes or applets to allow security levels to be tailored to the level of trust in the originator of the class or applet.

▶ Portable: Standard Java programs run with little or no change on a wide range of platforms. Perhaps surprisingly, there are more problems in running Java bytecode in the form of applets on some platforms, as discussed earlier in this unit. Portability often incurs a cost in terms of performance, but there are ways to limit the cost (see performance discussion below). Portability is normally a more valuable characteristic.

▶ High performance: This is a more doubtful claim – standard interpreted Java cannot really be described as high performance. However, specialized tools such as native compilers or JIT compilers can help achieve better performance where required and JIT compilation is standard in many current Java environments. Successive versions of the language have greatly improved the run-time performance of Java.

▶ Interpreted: We have seen that standard Java uses interpretation to achieve portability of bytecode. This has undoubtedly facilitated the widespread availability of Java, at some cost to run-time performance.

▶ Threaded: Java provides threads as part of the language, which makes this important feature relatively easy to use. There are, however, some platform-dependent variations in how threading works. We have also seen that Java threads are not sophisticated enough for specialized application areas such as real-time systems.

▶ Dynamic: Library classes can add new methods or instance variables without affecting programs that use these classes. It is easy to find out object types at run-time (for example, using `instanceof`) – this is particularly useful for some kinds of software tools, such as GUI builders, debuggers and plug-in components. Downloadable applets can also be considered a dynamic aspect of Java.

Overall, it seems that Java meets this list of aims well. However, there must be a slight suspicion that the designers wrote most of the detailed aims after they wrote the language!

8 Summary

In this unit, we have seen all the 'lets in Java technology – applets, MIDlets, servlets and aglets. We have also looked at how Java is being used in real-time systems and embedded devices, such as set-top boxes, and in smart cards, especially the Java Card standard.

A complex application will typically have a number of these different forms of Java technology, each component carrying out the role to which it is best suited.

The underlying theme of this course has been that Java is not only everywhere in the sense that it is a highly portable programming language, but also in the sense that it is able to run on a very wide range of platforms. Since its introduction in 1995, Java has established itself as a tremendously versatile and widely used programming language.

As to the future of Java, some commentators have suggested that Java may be around for another 20 to 30 years, if its evolution is managed carefully. Further versions of the Java language are still in the pipeline and there is a continuing focus on enhancing the language and the development tools to simplify the development process. A system known as the Java Community Process enables a very broad community of companies, researchers and others to contribute to the development of Java technology in a collaborative way. This should help to ensure the maintenance of one of Java's most successful features – its use of standards to ensure compatibility across the widest possible range of platforms. From the tiny wireless sensors known as 'smart dust' through to massive enterprise scale systems, it is likely that Java will continue to be 'everywhere' for quite some time to come.

This concludes the part of the course dealing with Java. The remainder of the course contains two case studies and you will be asked to study some aspects of these case studies.

LEARNING OUTCOMES

When you have completed this unit, you should be able to:

▶ write simple Java applets;

▶ write simple MIDlets for small-footprint devices to run on an emulator;

▶ explain the role of servlets and Java Server Pages in web applications;

▶ briefly describe Java software agents (aglets) and their uses;

▶ identify the uses of Java in embedded systems and smart cards;

▶ engage in further study of emerging Java applications and technologies.

Concepts

aglets, applets, CDC, CLDC, CGI, DBMS, high level user interface, HTTP, J2ME, Java Card, JAD, JAR, Java editions, Java-enabled browser, JDBC, JDBC driver, JSP (Java Server Pages), Just-in-time (JIT) compiler, low level user interface, MIDlets, MIDP, native compiler, real-time Java, real-time system, RTSJ, sandbox, scriptlet, server context, servlets, servlet container, signed applets, SQL, SQL query, thin client.

Index

A

agents 56

aglets 5, 56
   life cycle 58
   security 57
   server context 57

aims of Java language 67

applets 6–7, 10–12, 43, 56
   <APPLET> tag 8, 10
   <OBJECT> tag 10
   appletviewer 10
   browser versions 18
   JApplet 7
   life cycle 10–11
   sandbox model 16
   security 16
   signed applets 17

B

browsers 6–7, 9, 18
   browser versions 18

C

Canvas 36

CDC 21

CGI 43

CLDC 21

Command 29

CommandListener 23, 28, 30

commands 29

Common Gateway Interface 43

compilers 62
   Just-in-time 62
   native compilers 62

Connected Device
Configuration 21

Connected Limited Device
Configuration 21, 40
   Generic Connection
   Framework 40

connectivity 40

D

database access 54

database management system 54

Displayable 25
   class hierarchy 26

doPost method 50

E

embedded systems 60

F

Form 31

forms 49

G

Gauge 31

GCF 40

Generic Connection
Framework 40

H

high level interfaces 23, 25
   Form 31
   Screen 26
   TextBox 26

HTML forms 49

HTTP 40, 44
   POST 50

HttpServlet 45

I

ItemStateListener 33

J

J2EE 5, 43

J2ME 5, 20
   CDC 21
   CLDC 21
   configurations 21

J2SE 5

JAD files 41

JAR files 41

Java Card 65

Java editions 5

Java Server Pages 53

Java Technology concept map 67

Java Virtual Machine 6, 18, 21, 61

Java-enabled browser 8

JavaScript 17

JDBC 54

JIT 62

JSP 52–53

Just-in-time compilers 62

JVM 6

K

Kilobyte Virtual Machine (KVM) 21

L

low level interfaces 25, 36
   Canvas 36

M

MIDlets 5, 20
   CommandListener 23
   connectivity 40
   high level interface 23
   JAD files 41
   JAR files 41
   low level interfaces 36
   MIDlet class 23
   packaging 41
   persistent storage 40
   porting 41
   resource folder 33
   security 41
   states and transitions 23–24
   user interfaces 25

MIDP 21

mobile applications 20

Mobile Information Device
Profile 21, 40
   Record Management System 40

N

native compilers 62

P

PDAs 21

porting MIDlets 41

R

Real-time Specification for
Java 61

real-time systems 60

Record Management System 40

RTSJ 61

S
sandbox model 16, 57

Screen 26

scriptlets 53

security 16, 41, 43
  applets 16
  Java security manager 17
  sandbox model 16, 57

server context 57

servlets 5, 43
  and database access 54
  container 44
  doPost method 50
  HttpServlet 45
  security 43

set-top boxes 21, 63

signed applets 17

smart cards 65

SQL 54

T
TextBox 26

thin clients 43

Tomcat 44

W
web applications 43

web pages, forms 49